PRAISE FOR MICHAEL BA

From "*The Power of Regenerative Agriculture:*"

This is your go-to book to help inspire and educate yourself about the possibility of how you can play a role in the interconnection of farming systems with the entirety of the ecological system.

— D. G. FARNSWORTH

Well done book. I liked the chapter summaries at the end of each chapter. Chapter 6, was spot on in describing the challenges and barriers to implementing regenerative agriculture. The author has a passion for this subject and has provided very clear and concise data. The Afterword ends the book on a positive note and a view of hope that we'll get there.

— SRP

These guides to being environmentally responsible often come across as a little preachy. This is not one of those. It's informative and well-written, with a cheerful attitude toward ecologically friendly farming methods.

— LWHIT

PRACTICAL PERMACULTURE

A BEGINNER'S GUIDE TO DESIGNING A RESILIENT AND SUSTAINABLE GARDEN ECOSYSTEM FOR SELF-SUFFICIENT LIVING

SUSTAINABLE AGRICULTURE

MICHAEL BARTON

Book
Bound Studios

The information contained in this book is based on the author's personal experiences and research. While every effort has been made to ensure the accuracy of the information presented, the author and publisher cannot be held responsible for any errors or omissions.

This book is intended for general informational purposes only and is not a substitute for professional medical, legal, or financial advice. If you have specific questions about any medical, legal, or financial matters, you should consult with a qualified healthcare professional, attorney, or financial advisor.

Book Bound Studios is not affiliated with any product or vendor mentioned in this book. The views expressed in this book are those of the author and do not necessarily reflect the views of Book Bound Studios.

To the pioneers of permaculture, whose tireless quest for sustainability and balance has illuminated the path for so many, we express our deepest gratitude. Your commitment to regenerating our planet's ecosystems serves as a beacon of hope, inspiring each of us to become mindful stewards of the land we inhabit.

In nature's infinite book of secrecy, a little we can read.

— WILLIAM SHAKESPEARE

CONTENTS

INTRODUCTION

In today's fast-paced world, where convenience often takes precedence over sustainability, finding ways to live in harmony with our environment is more important than ever. One such approach is permaculture, a holistic design system that seeks to create sustainable human habitats by emulating the patterns and relationships found in nature. Practical permaculture is the application of these principles to our everyday lives, transforming our homes, gardens, and communities into thriving, resilient ecosystems.

The term "permaculture" is a combination of the words *"permanent" and "agriculture,"* reflecting the movement's origins in sustainable agriculture. However, permaculture has since evolved into various disciplines, including architecture, urban planning, and social systems. At its core, permaculture is about designing **systems that work with nature**, rather than against it, to meet our needs while preserving the planet's health.

In this chapter, we will introduce you to the world of practical permaculture, exploring its history, principles, and ethics. We will then delve into the key components of a permaculture system, from soil health and water management to plant selection and animal integration. Next, we will guide you through the process of designing your own permaculture garden, whether you have a small urban balcony or a sprawling rural property. Finally, we will share inspiring real-life examples and success stories from around the globe, demonstrating the transformative power of practical permaculture.

As you embark on this journey, you will discover that permaculture is more than just a set of gardening techniques; it is a mindset, a way of life that fosters a deep connection with the natural world and a sense of responsibility for its well-being. By embracing practical permaculture, you create a more sustainable future for yourself and your loved ones and contribute to the larger global movement towards a more just, equitable, and regenerative world. So let's get started, and welcome to the world of practical permaculture!

The Principles and Ethics of Permaculture

Permaculture is a holistic approach to sustainable living that integrates ecological design, resource conservation, and self-sufficiency. At the heart of permaculture are its principles and ethics, which serve as guidelines for creating harmonious, resilient, and productive systems that benefit both humans and the environment. This section will delve into these foundational concepts and explore how they can be applied practically to create thriving permaculture systems.

The Ethics of Permaculture

Permaculture is grounded in three core ethics that guide its practitioners in making responsible and sustainable choices. These ethics are:

Earth Care: This ethic emphasizes the importance of nurturing and preserving the planet's ecosystems, soil, water, and biodiversity. Earth care encourages us to consider the long-term consequences of our actions and to strive for practices that regenerate and enhance the environment.

People Care: This ethic fosters healthy, supportive, and resilient communities. People care encourages cooperation, sharing of resources, and prioritizing the well-being of all individuals. It also highlights the importance of personal growth, self-reliance, and empowerment.

Fair Share: This ethic promotes equitable distribution of resources and opportunities within human societies and between humans and other species. Fair sharing encourages us to limit our consumption, reduce waste, and share surplus resources with others in need.

The Principles of Permaculture

Permaculture principles, derived from observing natural ecosystems, provide practical guidance for designing and managing sustainable systems. While there are various interpretations of these principles, the following twelve are widely recognized and used by permaculture practitioners:

1. **Observe and Interact:** Careful observation of natural systems and thoughtful interaction with them allows us to learn from nature and adapt our practices accordingly.
2. **Catch and Store Energy:** Harnessing and storing renewable energy sources, such as sunlight, wind, and water, ensures a consistent supply of resources for our needs.
3. **Obtain a Yield:** Design systems that provide diverse and abundant resources, including food, energy, and materials, to meet our needs and support our well-being.
4. **Apply Self-Regulation and Accept Feedback:** Recognize the limits of our actions and adapt our practices based on the feedback we receive from our systems and the environment.
5. **Use and Value Renewable Resources and Services:** Prioritize using renewable resources and natural processes to minimize our dependence on non-renewable inputs.
6. **Produce No Waste:** Minimize waste by valuing and using all resources, recycling, and repurposing materials whenever possible.
7. **Design from Patterns to Details:** Observe patterns in nature and use them as a foundation for designing systems while also considering the unique details of each situation.

8. **Integrate Rather Than Segregate:** Create synergistic relationships between elements in a system, promoting cooperation, resource sharing, and mutual support.
9. **Use Small and Slow Solutions:** Emphasize small-scale, localized solutions that are more manageable, adaptable, and resilient over time.
10. **Use and Value Diversity:** Incorporate diverse elements, species, and strategies to create resilient systems that can withstand disturbances and adapt to change.
11. **Use Edges and Value the Marginal:** Recognize the potential in transitional areas and underutilized spaces where unique interactions and opportunities can occur.
12. **Creatively Use and Respond to Change:** Embrace change as an opportunity for growth and adaptation, and design systems that can evolve over time.

By understanding and applying these ethics and principles, we can create permaculture systems that are sustainable and regenerative, improving the health of our planet and our communities. In the following sections, we will explore the key components of a permaculture system and learn how to design and implement practical permaculture solutions in our own gardens and landscapes.

Key Components of a Permaculture System

Permaculture is a holistic approach to gardening and agriculture that seeks to create sustainable, self-sufficient ecosystems. To achieve this, permaculture systems incorporate a variety of key components that work together to create a harmonious and productive environment. In this section, we will explore some of the most important elements of a permaculture system and how they contribute to its overall success.

Zones and Sectors

One of the foundational concepts in permaculture is the idea of dividing your land into zones and sectors. Zones are garden or landscape areas organized by the frequency of human use and interaction. For example, Zone 1 might include the areas closest to your home, such as a kitchen garden or herb spiral, while Zone 5 might be a more remote area designated for wildlife habitat and minimal human intervention.

Sectors, on the other hand, are determined by the natural elements that influence your site, such as sunlight, wind, and water. By understanding these factors and designing your garden accordingly, you can maximize the efficiency and productivity of your permaculture system.

Plant Stacking and Polycultures

In a permaculture system, plants are strategically placed to maximize their benefits and minimize competition for resources. This is achieved through a technique called plant stacking, which involves layering plants vertically to create a diverse and productive ecosystem. For example, tall trees provide shade for understory plants, while groundcovers and root crops fill in the spaces below.

Polycultures, or the practice of growing multiple species together, also play a crucial role in permaculture systems. By planting a variety of crops, you can create a more resilient and productive garden that is less susceptible to pests and diseases.

Soil Health and Fertility

Healthy soil is the foundation of any successful permaculture system. You can support a diverse and productive ecosystem by focusing on building and maintaining soil fertility. Permaculture techniques for improving soil health include composting, mulching, and incorporating nitrogen-fixing plants into your garden design.

Water Management

Water is a precious resource, and permaculture systems aim to use it as efficiently as possible. This can be achieved through a variety of methods, such as capturing and storing rainwater, creating swales to slow and spread water across the landscape, and using drip irrigation systems to minimize water waste.

Animal Integration

Animals play a vital role in permaculture systems, providing valuable services such as pest control, soil aeration, and nutrient cycling. You can create a more balanced and productive ecosystem by incorporating animals into your garden design. Examples of animal integration include keeping chickens for pest control and egg production or incorporating a pond for fish and aquatic plants.

Energy Efficiency and Renewable Resources

Permaculture systems strive to minimize their reliance on non-renewable resources and instead focus on using energy and materials as efficiently as possible. This might include using solar panels for electricity, incorporating passive solar design principles into your home, or utilizing locally sourced and recycled materials for construction projects.

By understanding and incorporating these key components into your permaculture system, you can create a thriving and sustainable ecosystem that provides for your needs while benefiting the environment. As you continue to learn and experiment with permaculture techniques, you'll discover the incredible potential of this holistic approach to gardening and agriculture.

Designing Your Permaculture Garden

Embarking on the journey to create your own permaculture garden is exciting and rewarding. This section will guide you through the process of designing a garden that is both practical and sustainable while also being a beautiful and productive space. By following the principles and ethics of permaculture, you can create a garden that works in harmony with nature, providing you with an abundance of fresh produce and a thriving ecosystem.

Assessing Your Site

Before diving into the design process, it's essential to assess the unique characteristics of your site. This includes climate, topography, soil type, and available resources. By understanding the strengths and limitations of your site, you can make informed decisions about which plants and techniques will work best in your permaculture garden.

Begin by observing your site throughout the day and across different seasons. Take note of sun exposure, wind patterns, and water flow. This will help you determine the ideal placement for various garden elements, such as planting beds, water features, and windbreaks.

Zoning and Sector Analysis

In permaculture design, zoning is a technique used to organize your garden based on the frequency of human use and plant or animal needs. The zones are numbered from 1 to 5, with Zone 1 being the area closest to your home and Zone 5 being the furthest away.

- **Zone 1:** This area is visited daily and should include elements that require frequent attention, such as herbs, salad greens, and small fruit trees.
- **Zone 2:** This zone is visited less frequently and is suitable for larger fruit trees, vegetables, and small livestock.
- **Zone 3:** This area is used for larger-scale crop production and may include orchards, pasture, or grain fields.
- **Zone 4:** This zone is semi-wild and can be used for foraging, firewood production, and wildlife habitat.
- **Zone 5:** This area is left undisturbed as a natural ecosystem, providing a space for wildlife and natural processes to occur.

Sector analysis involves identifying external factors that may influence your garden, such as sun, wind, and water. By understanding these factors, you can design your garden to maximize positive influences and minimize negative ones.

Choosing Plants and Animals

When selecting plants and animals for your permaculture garden, consider their functions, needs, and relationships. Choose plants that serve multiple purposes, such as providing food, improving soil fertility, and attracting beneficial insects. Consider incorporating animals like chickens or bees to help with pest control, pollination, and nutrient cycling.

Creating a Garden Layout

With your site assessment, zoning, and plant selection complete, it's time to create a layout for your permaculture garden. Start by sketching a rough plan, placing elements based on their zone and sector requirements. Consider the relationships between plants and animals, ensuring each element supports and benefits from its neighbors.

Incorporate techniques such as swales, hugelkultur beds, and keyhole gardens to maximize water efficiency and soil fertility. Design pathways and access points to make it easy to maintain and harvest your garden.

Implementing and Adapting Your Design

Once your design is complete, it's time to bring your permaculture garden to life. Start by preparing the soil, adding organic matter, and creating planting beds. Next, plant your chosen species, taking care to provide them with the appropriate conditions for growth.

As your garden matures, observe and learn from its successes and challenges. Adapt your design as needed, making adjustments to improve productivity and sustainability. Remember that permaculture is an ongoing process, and your garden will evolve over time.

By following these steps, you can create a permaculture garden that is both practical and sustainable, providing you with an abundance of fresh produce and a thriving ecosystem. Embrace permaculture principles and enjoy the journey towards a more sustainable future.

Real-Life Examples and Success Stories

This section will explore some inspiring real-life examples and success stories of practical permaculture. These stories demonstrate the transformative power of permaculture principles when applied to various contexts, from urban gardens to rural farms. By examining these examples, we can gain valuable insights into the potential of permaculture to create sustainable, productive, and resilient systems that benefit both people and the planet.

The Urban Oasis: A Permaculture Garden in the City

Our first example takes us to the heart of the bustling city in *San Francisco*, where a small plot of land has been transformed into a thriving permaculture garden. This urban oasis demonstrates that even in the most densely populated areas, it is possible to create productive and sustainable green spaces.

The garden's design maximizes the use of vertical space by implementing trellises, arbors, and stacked planters. This allows for a diverse range of plants to be grown, including vegetables, herbs, and fruit trees. **Rainwater harvesting** systems and composting methods are employed to minimize waste and promote a closed-loop system. The garden also serves as a community hub where neighbors can come together to learn about permaculture, share resources, and enjoy the fruits of their labor.

The Regenerative Farm: Healing the Land and Building Community

Next, we visit a rural farm in *Missouri* that has embraced permaculture principles to regenerate degraded land and build a strong, resilient community. This farm's success story demonstrates the power of permaculture to heal ecosystems and foster social connections.

The farm has dramatically increased soil fertility, biodiversity, and overall productivity by implementing agroforestry, holistic grazing, and no-till farming practices. The farm also hosts workshops and educational programs, teaching others about the benefits of regenerative agriculture and permaculture design. By fostering a sense of community and shared responsibility, this farm has become a model for sustainable agriculture and rural development.

The Schoolyard Transformation: Educating the Next Generation

Our final example highlights the transformative power of permaculture in an educational setting. A once-barren schoolyard in *California* has been transformed into a vibrant permaculture garden, providing students with hands-on learning opportunities and a deeper connection to the natural world.

The garden incorporates a variety of permaculture design elements, including raised beds, companion planting, and a small-scale aquaponics system. Students are actively involved in the garden's maintenance and harvest, learning valuable skills in organic gardening, composting, and water conservation. The garden also serves as an outdoor classroom, where lessons in ecology, biology, and **environmental stewardship** come to life.

These real-life examples and success stories demonstrate the incredible potential of practical permaculture to create positive change in diverse settings. By applying the principles and ethics of permaculture, we can design systems that not only provide for our needs but also regenerate ecosystems, build community, and foster a more sustainable future for all.

Embracing a Sustainable Future with Practical Permaculture

As we reach the end of this brief introduction to the world of practical permaculture, it is important to reflect on the powerful impact that this holistic approach to gardening and land management can have on our lives, our communities, and our planet. By embracing the principles and ethics of permaculture, we can create sustainable, resilient, and abundant systems that not only provide for our needs but also contribute to the healing and regeneration of our environment.

To conclude, let us remember the words of permaculture co-founder *Bill Mollison: "Though the problems of the world are increasingly complex, the solutions remain embarrassingly simple."* By applying the wisdom of practical permaculture, we can be part of the solution and help create a world where all living beings can thrive.

1

UNDERSTANDING PERMACULTURE PRINCIPLES

A flourishing permaculture garden with diverse plants and wildlife.

Permaculture is a holistic approach to designing sustainable systems that work in harmony with nature. It is a practical and ethical framework that aims to create **resilient**, **self-sufficient**, and **regenerative environments**. In this chapter, we will delve into the core principles of permaculture, which serve as a foundation for designing and implementing sustainable systems in various aspects of our lives.

The concept of permaculture was developed in the *1970s* by Australian ecologists Bill Mollison and David Holmgren. They sought to create a solution to the growing environmental and social challenges of their time, such as soil erosion, deforestation, and resource depletion. Permaculture is not just about growing food; it is a comprehensive approach encompassing various aspects of human life, including housing, energy, water management, and community development.

At the heart of permaculture lie its principles, which provide a set of guidelines for designing sustainable systems. These principles are derived from observing and understanding the patterns and relationships found in nature. By mimicking these natural processes, we can create systems that are not only sustainable but also regenerative, meaning they improve the environment and the quality of life for all living beings.

In this chapter, we will explore the ethics and principles of permaculture, which serve as a foundation for its practice. First, we will discuss the three core ethics of permaculture: Earth Care, People Care, and Fair Share, which guide our actions and decisions in creating sustainable systems. We will then delve into the twelve design principles of permaculture, which provide a framework for designing and implementing these systems in various aspects of our lives.

Furthermore, we will discuss how to apply permaculture principles in everyday life, from our homes and gardens to our communities and workplaces. We will also explore real-world examples of permaculture in action, showcasing the incredible potential of this approach to create positive change in the world.

By understanding and embracing permaculture principles, we can work towards a more sustainable, resilient, and regenerative future for ourselves, our communities, and the planet as a whole. So, let's embark on this journey together and discover the power of permaculture to transform our lives and the world around us.

The Ethics of Permaculture: Earth Care, People Care, and Fair Share

At the heart of permaculture lies a set of three core ethics that serve as guiding principles for designing sustainable systems. These ethics - Earth Care, People Care, and Fair Share - are not only essential for the success of permaculture projects but also for fostering a sense of responsibility and interconnectedness among individuals and communities. In this section, we will delve into each of these ethics and explore their significance in the realm of permaculture.

Earth Care: Nurturing Our Planet

The first ethic, Earth Care, emphasizes the importance of protecting and preserving our planet's ecosystems, natural resources, and biodiversity. This ethic encourages us to adopt practices that regenerate and enhance the environment rather than deplete or harm it. By nurturing the earth, we ensure it remains a thriving and bountiful home for all living beings.

Earth Care is practiced in permaculture by designing systems that work in harmony with nature rather than against it. This includes using renewable resources, minimizing waste, and promoting biodiversity. For example, a permaculture garden may incorporate plants that attract beneficial insects, create habitat for wildlife, and improve soil fertility, all while providing food and other resources for humans.

People Care: Supporting Our Communities

The second ethic, People Care, focuses on the well-being of individuals and communities. Permaculture recognizes that the health of our planet is inextricably linked to the health of its inhabitants. By fostering solid and resilient communities, we create a support network that can better withstand the challenges of a changing world.

People Care is practiced in permaculture by designing systems that meet the needs of all community members, including access to healthy food, clean water, and safe shelter. Additionally, permaculture encourages sharing knowledge and skills, empowering individuals to become active participants in their own well-being and that of their community. This can be achieved through workshops, skill-sharing events, and community projects that bring people together to learn and grow.

Fair Share: Distributing Resources Equitably

The third ethic, Fair Share, is centered on the equitable distribution of resources and opportunities. This ethic acknowledges that our planet's resources are finite, and we must use them wisely to ensure that all living beings can thrive. By embracing the concept of "**enough,**" we can create systems that provide for everyone without exceeding the earth's carrying capacity.

In permaculture, Fair Share is practiced by designing systems that minimize consumption and waste while maximizing the use of available resources. This may involve using energy-efficient technologies, repurposing materials, and sharing surplus resources with others. For example, a permaculture community might establish a tool-sharing program, allowing members to access tools and equipment without the need for each individual to purchase their own.

By understanding and embracing the ethics of Earth Care, People Care, and Fair Share, we can create permaculture systems that provide for our needs and contribute to the well-being of our planet and its inhabitants. In addition, these ethics serve as a foundation for sustainable living, inspiring us to cultivate a deeper connection with the earth and each other.

The Twelve Design Principles of Permaculture

Permaculture is a holistic approach to sustainable living, integrating various elements of ecology, agriculture, and community design. At the heart of permaculture are twelve design principles that serve as a guide for creating harmonious, resilient, and productive systems. These principles, developed by permaculture co-founder David Holmgren, can be applied to any scale, from a small backyard garden to an entire community or ecosystem. Let's explore each of these principles and understand their significance in permaculture design.

1. **Observe and Interact:** The first principle emphasizes the importance of observation and engagement with the natural environment. By carefully observing and understanding the patterns, relationships, and interactions within a system, we can make informed decisions and design solutions that are in harmony with nature.

2. **Catch and Store Energy:** This principle encourages us to capture and store energy in various forms, such as water, sunlight, and biomass. By doing so, we can create a reserve of resources that can be utilized during times of scarcity or need.

3. **Obtain a Yield:** Permaculture systems should be designed to provide for our needs, whether food, shelter, or other resources. We can create a sustainable and self-reliant system by ensuring we obtain a yield from our efforts.

4. **Apply Self-Regulation and Accept Feedback:** This principle highlights the importance of creating systems that are self-regulating and responsive to feedback. By designing systems that can adapt and evolve, we can minimize the need for external inputs and reduce the risk of system failure.

5. **Use and Value Renewable Resources and Services:** Permaculture encourages the use of renewable resources and natural services, such as solar energy, wind power, and natural pest control. Utilizing these resources can reduce our dependence on non-renewable resources and minimize our ecological footprint.

6. **Produce No Waste:** This principle emphasizes the importance of minimizing waste and utilizing resources efficiently. By designing systems

that recycle and reuse materials, we can create a closed-loop system that mimics the efficiency of natural ecosystems.

7. **Design from Patterns to Details:** Permaculture design starts with understanding the larger patterns and relationships within a system and then moves toward the specific details. By focusing on the broader context, we can create more resilient and adaptable systems.

8. **Integrate Rather Than Segregate:** In permaculture, elements within a system are designed to work together and support one another. We can create a more efficient and harmonious system by creating connections and fostering relationships between different components.

9. **Use Small and Slow Solutions:** This principle encourages us to focus on small-scale, manageable solutions that can be implemented gradually over time. By starting small and building upon our successes, we can create lasting change and minimize the risk of failure.

10. **Use and Value Diversity:** Diversity is a key component of resilient systems, as it provides redundancy and increases the overall stability of a system. By incorporating a variety of plants, animals, and strategies, we can create a more adaptable and resilient system.

11. **Use Edges and Value the Marginal:** In permaculture, the edges and marginal areas of a system are often the most productive and diverse. By focusing on these areas and utilizing their unique characteristics, we can create innovative solutions and maximize the potential of our systems.

12. **Creatively Use and Respond to Change:** Change is an inevitable part of life, and permaculture encourages us to embrace and adapt to these changes. By being flexible and responsive, we can turn challenges into opportunities and create systems that are resilient in the face of uncertainty.

By understanding and applying these twelve design principles, we can create permaculture systems that are not only sustainable but also regenerative, improving the health of our environment and the well-being of our communities. The following sections will explore how these principles can be applied in everyday life and examine real-world examples of permaculture in action.

Applying Permaculture Principles in Everyday Life

Incorporating permaculture principles into your everyday life may seem daunting, but it doesn't have to be. By making small, conscious changes and adopting a permaculture mindset, you can create a more sustainable and harmonious lifestyle. This section will explore practical ways to apply permaculture principles in your daily life, making it easier for you to embrace these concepts and contribute to a more sustainable future.

To begin with, let's consider the three ethics of permaculture: Earth Care, People Care, and Fair Share. These ethics can guide your actions and decisions in various aspects of your life, from the food you eat to the way you interact with your community. Here are some suggestions for incorporating these ethics into your daily routine:

Earth Care: Make an effort to reduce your ecological footprint by conserving resources, reducing waste, and supporting local, organic, and sustainable products. This can include simple actions like turning off lights when not in use, recycling, and composting your food waste. Additionally, consider growing your own food or supporting local farmers' markets to promote sustainable agriculture.

People Care: Foster a sense of community and connection by participating in local events, volunteering, or joining a community garden. You can create a supportive network that values collaboration and mutual aid by nurturing relationships with those around you.

Fair Share: Practice mindful consumption by being aware of the impact your choices have on the environment and other people. This can involve reducing your consumption of non-essential items, sharing resources with others, and supporting businesses that prioritize ethical and sustainable practices.

Next, let's explore how you can apply the twelve design principles of permaculture in your everyday life:

1. **Observe and interact:** Pay attention to the natural patterns and cycles around you, such as the changing seasons, local wildlife, and weather patterns. This awareness can help you make informed decisions about your lifestyle and surroundings.

2. **Catch and store energy:** Utilize renewable energy sources, such as

solar panels or wind turbines, to power your home. Additionally, consider insulating your home to conserve energy and reduce heating and cooling costs.

3. **Obtain a yield:** Grow your own food or support local agriculture to ensure a sustainable and nutritious food supply.

4. **Apply self-regulation and accept feedback:** Continuously evaluate and adjust your actions and choices based on their impact on the environment and your community.

5. **Use and value renewable resources and services:** Prioritize the use of renewable resources, such as solar power, rainwater harvesting, and sustainable materials in your home and garden.

6. **Produce no waste:** Adopt a zero-waste mindset by reducing, reusing, and recycling materials whenever possible.

7. **Design from patterns to details:** Observe the patterns in nature and apply them to your home, garden, and community to create a harmonious and efficient environment.

8. **Integrate rather than segregate:** Foster connections between different elements of your life, such as incorporating edible plants into your landscaping or inviting neighbors to participate in a community garden.

9. **Use small and slow solutions:** Focus on making incremental changes and adopting sustainable practices over time rather than seeking immediate and drastic transformations.

10. **Use and value diversity:** Embrace the unique qualities of your local environment, culture, and community by incorporating diverse plants, animals, and traditions into your lifestyle.

11. **Use edges and value the marginal:** Recognize the potential of underutilized spaces, such as vacant lots or neglected areas in your community, and transform them into productive and vibrant spaces.

12. **Creatively use and respond to change:** Embrace change as an opportunity for growth and adaptation, and be open to new ideas and perspectives.

Integrating these permaculture principles into your daily life can create a more sustainable, resilient, and fulfilling lifestyle. As you continue to learn and grow, you'll find that the benefits of permaculture extend far beyond your own backyard, contributing to a healthier and more harmonious world for all.

Permaculture in Action: Real-World Examples

As we delve deeper into the world of permaculture, it's essential to see how these principles can be applied in real-life situations. By examining various examples from around the globe, we can better understand how permaculture practices can be adapted to different environments and cultures. In this section, we will explore a few inspiring real-world examples that showcase the power of permaculture in action.

The Greening the Desert Project, Jordan

The Greening the Desert Project, located in the arid region of Jordan, is a testament to the transformative power of permaculture. This project, led by permaculture expert Geoff Lawton, has successfully turned a barren landscape into a thriving food forest. By implementing permaculture principles such as water harvesting, soil regeneration, and planting a diverse range of edible plants, the project has created a sustainable ecosystem that provides food, shelter, and income for the local community.

The Bullock Brothers Homestead, USA

The Bullock Brothers Homestead, located on Orcas Island in Washington State, is a prime example of a successful permaculture farm. For over 30 years, the Bullock brothers have been applying permaculture principles to their 25-acre property, resulting in a lush, productive landscape. The farm features a diverse array of plants, animals, and natural building techniques, all working together to create a self-sustaining ecosystem. In addition, the Bullock Brothers Homestead serves as an educational center, inspiring visitors to embrace permaculture principles in their own lives.

The Chikukwa Project, Zimbabwe

In the remote region of Chikukwa, Zimbabwe, a community-led permaculture project has transformed the lives of over 7,000 people. Faced with deforestation, soil erosion, and food scarcity, the Chikukwa community adopted permaculture principles to restore their land and improve their livelihoods. Through a combination of agroforestry, water management, and organic farming techniques, the Chikukwa Project has increased crop yields, improved food security, and empowered the community to become more self-reliant.

Incredible Edible, UK

Incredible Edible is a grassroots movement that began in the small town of Todmorden, UK. The initiative encourages residents to grow food in public spaces like parks, sidewalks, and even outside the police station. By embracing the permaculture principle of "people care," Incredible Edible has fostered a strong sense of community and connection to the local environment. The movement has since spread to over 100 communities worldwide, demonstrating the power of permaculture to inspire positive change on a global scale.

These real-world examples illustrate the incredible potential of permaculture to transform our landscapes, communities, and lives. By applying the principles of permaculture in our gardens, homes, and neighborhoods, we can contribute to a more sustainable and resilient future for our planet.

Embracing Permaculture for a Sustainable Future

As we reach the end of this chapter, it is essential to reflect on the significance of these principles and their potential to reshape our future. The beauty of permaculture lies in its simplicity, adaptability, and the fact that it is rooted in the natural world. By embracing these principles, we can create a more sustainable, resilient, and harmonious environment for ourselves and future generations.

The ethics of permaculture - Earth Care, People Care, and Fair Share - serve as a guiding compass, reminding us of our responsibility to protect the planet, nurture our communities, and promote equitable distribution of resources. These ethics are not just applicable to gardening or agriculture; they can be integrated into every aspect of our lives, from our homes and workplaces to our relationships and personal choices.

The Twelve Design Principles of Permaculture provide a practical framework for implementing these ethics in our daily lives. We can create efficient, productive, and self-sustaining systems by observing and interacting with our environment, catching and storing energy, obtaining a yield, and applying self-regulation and feedback. Furthermore, by using and valuing renewable resources, producing no waste, and designing from patterns to details, we can minimize our ecological footprint and maximize our positive impact on the planet.

Applying permaculture principles in everyday life may seem daunting at first, but it is essential to remember that small, incremental changes can lead to significant transformations. Start by making conscious choices in your home, such as reducing waste, conserving water, and growing your own food. Then, as you gain confidence and experience, you can expand your permaculture practices to your community, workplace, and beyond.

In conclusion, embracing permaculture for a sustainable future is a viable and necessary option. As we face unprecedented environmental challenges, it is crucial that we adopt practices that promote ecological balance, social equity, and economic stability. By incorporating permaculture principles into our lives, we can become active participants in creating a more sustainable, resilient, and harmonious world. So, let us embark on this journey together, guided by the wisdom of nature and the power of permaculture, and leave a lasting legacy for generations to come.

Chapter Summary

- Permaculture is a holistic approach to designing sustainable systems that work in harmony with nature, encompassing various aspects of human life, including housing, energy, water management, and community development.
- The three core ethics of permaculture are Earth Care, People Care, and Fair Share, which guide our actions and decisions in creating sustainable systems.
- The Twelve Design Principles of Permaculture provide a practical framework for implementing sustainable practices in various aspects of our lives.
- Permaculture principles can be applied in everyday life through small, conscious changes, such as reducing waste, conserving water, and growing your own food.
- The ethics and principles of permaculture can be integrated into every aspect of our lives, from our homes and workplaces to our relationships and personal choices.
- Real-world examples of permaculture in action demonstrate its incredible versatility and effectiveness in diverse settings across the globe.
- Embracing permaculture for a sustainable future is not only a viable option but a necessary one as we face unprecedented environmental challenges.
- By incorporating permaculture principles into our lives, we can become active participants in creating a more sustainable, resilient, and harmonious world for future generations.

2

DESIGNING YOUR PERMACULTURE GARDEN

A permaculture garden brimming with life, where diverse plants and vegetables grow harmoniously alongside each other, creating a lush green tapestry.

Welcome to the exciting journey of designing your very own permaculture garden! This chapter aims to guide you through the essential steps of creating a sustainable, productive, and beautiful space that works in harmony with nature. By embracing the principles of permaculture, you will not only enhance your garden's resilience and productivity but also contribute to a healthier planet.

Designing a permaculture garden is a creative and rewarding process that requires careful observation, planning, and implementation. The key to success lies in understanding the unique characteristics of your site and selecting the right combination of plants, animals, and sustainable techniques that work together to create a thriving ecosystem.

In this chapter, we will explore the following essential steps in designing your permaculture garden:

1. **Assessing Your Site and Its Resources:** Before you start designing your garden, it's crucial to understand the unique features and resources of your site. This section will guide you through the process of analyzing your soil, climate, water availability, and other factors that will influence your garden's design.

2. **Choosing the Right Plants and Animals for Your Garden:** Selecting the right combination of plants and animals is at the heart of permaculture design. This section will help you choose species that are well-suited to your site's conditions and that support each other in a mutually beneficial way.

3. **Integrating Sustainable Techniques and Systems:** Permaculture gardens are designed to be low-maintenance and self-sufficient. This section will introduce you to a range of sustainable techniques and systems that can help you conserve water, build soil fertility, and reduce waste in your garden.

4. **Creating a Maintenance Plan for Long-Term Success:** A well-designed permaculture garden should require minimal intervention to thrive. This section will provide guidance on creating a maintenance plan that ensures the long-term health and productivity of your garden.

5. **Bringing Your Permaculture Garden to Life:** Finally, we will wrap

up the chapter with some tips and inspiration for transforming your garden design into a living, breathing permaculture paradise.

By following these steps and embracing the principles of permaculture, you will be well on your way to creating a garden that is not only beautiful and productive but also a shining example of sustainability and harmony with nature. So, let's dive in and start designing your permaculture garden!

Assessing Your Site and Its Resources

Before diving into the exciting world of permaculture design, it is crucial to take a step back and **assess the unique characteristics of your site**. This will help you make informed decisions and ensure your permaculture garden is tailored to your specific environment. This section will discuss the key aspects to consider when evaluating your site and its resources.

First and foremost, take note of the size and shape of your garden. This will determine the scale of your permaculture project and influence the layout of your design. Next, sketch a rough map of your site, marking any existing structures, pathways, and vegetation. This will serve as a helpful reference throughout the design process.

Next, observe the natural elements of your site, such as sunlight, wind, and water. Identify the sunniest and shadiest areas and the direction of prevailing winds. This information will guide your plant and animal selections and the placement of key elements like windbreaks and water catchment systems.

Soil quality is another crucial factor to consider. Conduct a simple soil test to determine the texture, pH, and nutrient levels of your garden's soil. This will help you identify any amendments needed to create a fertile and productive growing environment. Additionally, observe any existing drainage patterns and consider how they may impact your design.

Take a moment to appreciate the biodiversity of your site. Are there native plants, insects, or animals that already call your garden home? These species can be valuable allies in your permaculture journey, contributing to pest control, pollination, and soil health. Make a list of these existing resources and consider how they can be integrated into your design.

Finally, assess the human and material resources available to you. Consider your skills, knowledge, time, and the support of friends, family, or neighbors who may be interested in collaborating on your permaculture project. Additionally, take stock of any materials you already have on hand, such as compost, mulch, or tools. These resources can reduce the overall cost of your project and contribute to its sustainability.

In conclusion, assessing your site and its resources is vital in designing a thriving permaculture garden. By understanding the unique characteristics of your environment and harnessing the power of available resources, you can create a thriving ecosystem that is both productive and sustainable.

Choosing the Right Plants and Animals for Your Garden

Selecting the appropriate plants and animals for your permaculture garden is a crucial step in ensuring its success. By carefully considering the needs and characteristics of each species, you can create a thriving ecosystem that benefits both you and the environment. In this section, we will explore the factors to consider when choosing plants and animals for your garden, as well as some popular choices for permaculture enthusiasts.

When selecting plants for your permaculture garden, it's essential to consider the following factors:

Climate and microclimate: Choose plants that are well-suited to your region's climate and the specific microclimate of your garden. This will ensure that your plants can thrive without excessive intervention or the need for artificial heating or cooling.

Soil type and fertility: Different plants have varying preferences for soil type and fertility levels. By selecting plants that are well-suited to your garden's soil conditions, you can minimize the need for soil amendments and fertilizers.

Sunlight and shade: Consider the amount of sunlight and shade available in your garden when selecting plants. Some plants require full sun, while others prefer partial shade or even full shade.

Water requirements: Choose plants with water requirements that match the natural rainfall patterns in your area, as well as the water resources available in your garden. This will help to minimize the need for supplemental irrigation.

Plant relationships: In a permaculture garden, plants are chosen for their individual characteristics and ability to interact positively with other plants and animals. Consider selecting plants that can provide multiple functions, such as nitrogen-fixing legumes, insect-attracting flowers, or plants that provide food and habitat for beneficial animals.

Some popular plant choices for permaculture gardens include fruit and nut trees, berry bushes, perennial vegetables, herbs, and edible flowers. These plants can provide food, medicine, and other resources while also contributing to a healthy and diverse ecosystem.

In addition to plants, incorporating animals into your permaculture garden can provide numerous benefits, such as pest control, soil fertility, and food production. When selecting animals for your garden, consider the following factors:

Size and space requirements: Choose animals that are appropriate for the size of your garden and the available space. For example, small gardens may be better suited to chickens or rabbits, while larger gardens may be able to accommodate goats or sheep.

Dietary needs: Consider the dietary needs of the animals you choose and ensure that your garden can provide adequate food resources. For example, chickens can forage for insects and plants, while goats and sheep require access to pasture or browse.

Compatibility with plants and other animals: Select animals that can coexist peacefully with your plants and other animals in the garden. For example, ducks can be an excellent addition to a garden with a pond, as they can help control pests and algae while also providing eggs and meat.

Local regulations and restrictions: Be sure to research any regulations or restrictions on keeping animals in your area before adding them to your permaculture garden.

Some popular animal choices for permaculture gardens include chickens, ducks, bees, rabbits, and even small livestock like goats and sheep. By carefully selecting the right plants and animals for your garden, you can create a thriving, sustainable ecosystem that provides abundant resources for you and your family.

Integrating Sustainable Techniques and Systems

Creating a thriving permaculture garden involves more than just selecting the right plants and animals. It requires integrating sustainable techniques and systems that work in harmony with nature, ensuring your garden's long-term health and productivity. This section will explore some of the most effective and widely-used sustainable practices that can be easily incorporated into your permaculture design.

Water Conservation and Management: One of the core principles of permaculture is to use resources efficiently, and water is no exception. You can significantly reduce your garden's reliance on external water sources by implementing rainwater harvesting, swales, and mulching strategies. Additionally, consider incorporating drought-tolerant plants and using greywater recycling systems to further minimize water waste.

Soil Health and Fertility: Healthy soil is the foundation of a thriving permaculture garden. To maintain and improve soil fertility, incorporate organic matter through composting, cover cropping, and the use of green manures. These practices add essential nutrients to the soil and improve its structure and water retention capacity. Furthermore, avoid tilling the soil, as this can disrupt the natural balance of microorganisms and lead to soil compaction.

Policulture and Plant Diversity: Planting diverse species in your garden promotes a more resilient and productive ecosystem. Polyculture, or growing multiple species together, can help reduce pests and diseases, improve soil fertility, and create a more visually appealing landscape. When selecting plants for your garden, consider their various functions, such as nitrogen-fixing, pollinator-attracting, or pest-repelling properties.

Natural Pest Management: Chemical pesticides can harm both the environment and the beneficial organisms in your garden. Instead, opt for natural pest management techniques, such as companion planting, attracting predatory insects, and using physical barriers like row covers. Additionally, maintaining a healthy garden through proper plant selection and care can help to prevent pest problems in the first place.

Renewable Energy Sources: Integrating renewable energy sources into your permaculture garden can help to reduce your reliance on fossil fuels and minimize your ecological footprint. Solar panels, wind turbines, and small-scale hydroelectric systems are all viable options for generating clean, sustainable energy. Additionally, consider using energy-efficient tools and appliances, such as solar-powered water pumps or LED lighting.

Waste Reduction and Recycling: In a permaculture garden, waste is viewed as a valuable resource rather than something to be discarded. Implementing strategies such as composting, worm farming, and using plant-based mulches can help recycle organic waste into the garden. Additionally, consider repurposing materials like pallets, tires, or old containers for use in garden structures or as planters.

By incorporating these sustainable techniques and systems into your permaculture garden design, you can create a resilient, productive, and environmentally-friendly space that will thrive for years to come. Remember, the key to successful permaculture is to observe and learn from nature, adapting and refining your practices as your garden evolves.

Creating a Maintenance Plan for Long-Term Success

A flourishing permaculture garden is a living testament to the power of sustainable design and ecological harmony. However, even the most well-designed garden requires ongoing care and attention to ensure its long-term success. This section will explore the essential components of a maintenance plan that will keep your permaculture garden thriving for years to come.

First and foremost, it's crucial to remember that a permaculture garden is a **dynamic ecosystem** constantly evolving and adapting to changing conditions. As such, your maintenance plan should be flexible and responsive to your garden's needs. Regular observation and interaction with your garden will help you identify any issues that may arise and address them promptly.

One of the critical aspects of permaculture maintenance is managing the growth and spread of plants. This includes pruning, thinning, and harvesting to ensure your plants remain healthy and productive. For example, fruit trees may require annual pruning to encourage new growth and prevent overcrowding, while perennial plants may need to be divided and replanted to maintain vigor. Regularly harvesting your garden's bounty not only provides you with fresh, nutritious food but also helps to keep plants in check and prevent them from becoming too dominant.

Another vital component of a permaculture maintenance plan is soil health. Healthy soil is the foundation of a thriving garden, and monitoring and maintaining its fertility and structure is essential. This can be achieved through regular mulching, composting, and the use of cover crops to protect and nourish the soil. Additionally, rotating your crops and incorporating a diverse range of plants will help to prevent nutrient depletion and the buildup of pests and diseases.

Pest and disease management is also an important aspect of permaculture maintenance. In a well-designed garden, natural predators and beneficial insects will help to keep pests in check. However, it's still essential to monitor your garden for signs of infestation or disease and take appropriate action when necessary. This may include introducing additional beneficial insects, using organic pest control methods, or adjusting your planting strategies to reduce the risk of disease.

Water management is another critical factor in maintaining a successful permaculture garden. Ensuring that your plants receive the right amount of water – not too much or too little – is crucial for their health and productivity. This may involve adjusting your irrigation systems, collecting rainwater, or implementing water-saving techniques such as mulching and planting drought-tolerant species.

Finally, a long-term maintenance plan should also consider the ongoing evolution and development of your permaculture garden. As your garden matures, you may need to reassess its design and make adjustments to accommodate changing conditions or new goals. This could involve introducing new plants or animals, expanding your garden's size, or incorporating additional sustainable techniques and systems.

In conclusion, creating a maintenance plan for your permaculture garden ensures its long-term success. By regularly monitoring and caring for your garden, you can enjoy the many benefits of a thriving, sustainable ecosystem that provides nourishment, beauty, and inspiration for years to come.

Bringing Your Permaculture Garden to Life

As we reach the end of this chapter, it is time to take a step back and appreciate the incredible journey you have embarked upon in designing your permaculture garden. By now, you should have a solid understanding of the principles and techniques that will help you create a thriving, sustainable, and resilient ecosystem right in your backyard.

Throughout this chapter, we have explored the importance of assessing your site and its resources, selecting the right plants and animals for your garden, integrating sustainable techniques and systems, and creating a maintenance plan for long-term success. Each of these elements plays a crucial role in bringing your permaculture garden to life.

As you begin to implement your design, remember that **permaculture is not a one-size-fits-all approach**. It is a dynamic and adaptive process that encourages experimentation and learning from experience. Embrace the challenges and surprises that may arise along the way, as they will only deepen your understanding of the intricate relationships within your garden's ecosystem.

One of the most rewarding aspects of permaculture is witnessing the transformation of your garden as it evolves into a self-sustaining, productive, and biodiverse haven. With time, patience, and dedication, you will see the fruits of your labor as your garden becomes a living testament to the power of permaculture principles.

As you nurture your permaculture garden, you cultivate a healthier and more sustainable environment for yourself and your community and contribute to the **global movement** toward a more resilient and regenerative future. Your garden is a small but significant piece of the larger puzzle, and your efforts will inspire others to embark on their own permaculture journey.

In conclusion, designing and bringing your permaculture garden to life is exciting and fulfilling. As you continue to learn, adapt, and grow alongside your garden, you will undoubtedly experience the profound satisfaction of living in harmony with nature. So, go forth and cultivate your permaculture paradise, knowing that you are making a lasting, positive impact on the world around you.

Chapter Summary

- Permaculture is a holistic approach to gardening that focuses on creating sustainable, self-sufficient systems that work in harmony with nature.
- Assessing your site and its resources is crucial for understanding your garden's unique features and resources, which will influence its design.
- Choosing the right plants and animals for your garden is essential for creating a thriving ecosystem that benefits both you and the environment.
- Integrating sustainable techniques and systems, such as water conservation, soil health, and natural pest management, is key to creating a resilient and environmentally-friendly permaculture garden.
- A maintenance plan is necessary to ensure your permaculture garden's long-term success, including managing plant growth, soil health, pest and disease management, and water management.
- Permaculture is a dynamic and adaptive process that encourages experimentation and learning from experience, allowing for adjustments and improvements over time.

- Witnessing the transformation of your garden into a self-sustaining, productive, and biodiverse haven is one of the most rewarding aspects of permaculture.
- By cultivating a permaculture garden, you contribute to a global movement towards a more resilient and regenerative future, inspiring others to embark on their own permaculture journey.

3

SOIL HEALTH AND REGENERATION TECHNIQUES

A thriving garden with a variety of colorful plants and flowers, where the soil is visibly rich and healthy, with earthworms and microorganisms working together to regenerate the soil.

In the world of permaculture, the foundation of a thriving ecosystem lies in the health of its soil. Soil health and regeneration are essential components of sustainable agriculture and play a critical role in maintaining the balance of life on Earth. This chapter delves into the fascinating world of soil health and regeneration, exploring its importance in permaculture and providing practical techniques to nurture and restore this vital resource.

Soil is much more than just dirt; it is a complex, living ecosystem teeming with microorganisms, nutrients, and minerals that support plant growth and provide a habitat for countless organisms. Healthy soil is the backbone of a productive permaculture garden, as it supports the growth of diverse plant species, aids in water retention, and helps to regulate the climate. Unfortunately, conventional agricultural practices have led to widespread soil degradation, resulting in reduced fertility, erosion, and the loss of valuable topsoil.

In response to these challenges, permaculture offers a holistic approach to soil health and regeneration that emphasizes working with nature rather than against it. By understanding the intricacies of soil composition and implementing regenerative techniques, permaculture practitioners can create a thriving, resilient ecosystem that supports both human needs and the environment.

In this chapter, we will explore the importance of soil composition and its role in supporting a healthy permaculture system. We will discuss natural soil regeneration techniques that can be easily incorporated into your permaculture garden, as well as specific permaculture practices that promote soil health. Finally, we will provide guidance on monitoring and maintaining soil health, ensuring the lasting success of your permaculture endeavors.

So, let us embark on this journey to better understand the complex world beneath our feet and learn how to harness the power of healthy soil to create a thriving, sustainable permaculture garden.

Understanding Soil Composition and Its Importance

Soil is the foundation of any thriving permaculture garden. Therefore, understanding its composition is crucial for creating a sustainable and productive ecosystem. In this section, we will delve into the components of soil, the roles they play in supporting plant life, and why maintaining a healthy soil composition is essential for successful permaculture.

Soil is a complex and dynamic mixture of organic matter, minerals, water, air, and countless microorganisms. These components work together to create a living, breathing ecosystem that supports plant growth and contributes to the overall health of our environment. So let's take a closer look at each component and its role in **soil health.**

Organic matter: This includes decomposing plant and animal material, such as leaves, branches, and manure. As these materials break down, they release essential nutrients into the soil, which plants can then absorb through their roots. Organic matter also helps to improve soil structure, making it more porous and allowing air and water to circulate more easily.

Minerals: Soil contains various minerals, such as sand, silt, and clay, which provide essential nutrients for plant growth. The proportions of these minerals in the soil determine its texture, which in turn affects its ability to retain water and nutrients. A well-balanced soil composition will have a mix of all three mineral types, providing an ideal environment for plant growth.

Water: Soil moisture is vital for plant growth, as it dissolves and transports nutrients to the plant roots. Water also plays a crucial role in maintaining the soil's structure. It helps bind particles together and creates a stable environment for plant roots to anchor themselves.

Air: Oxygen is essential for the survival of both plants and soil-dwelling microorganisms. A well-aerated soil allows plant roots to access the oxygen they need for respiration while also providing a hospitable environment for beneficial microbes to thrive.

Microorganisms: Soil is teeming with billions of microscopic organisms, including bacteria, fungi, and protozoa. These tiny creatures play a vital role in breaking down organic matter, recycling nutrients, and maintaining soil structure. They also help to protect plants from diseases and pests by competing with harmful organisms and producing natural antibiotics.

Understanding the importance of each component in soil composition is the first step toward creating a healthy and productive permaculture garden. By nurturing and maintaining a well-balanced soil ecosystem, you can ensure your plants have access to the nutrients, water, and air they need to grow strong and resilient. This will lead to a more sustainable and self-sufficient garden, with minimal need for external inputs and reduced reliance on synthetic fertilizers and pesticides. In the next section, we will explore natural soil regeneration techniques that can help you achieve this goal.

Natural Soil Regeneration Techniques

In this section, we will delve into the world of natural soil regeneration techniques that can be easily incorporated into your permaculture garden. These methods not only help improve soil health but also contribute to the overall sustainability of your garden's ecosystem. By understanding and implementing these techniques, you will be taking a significant step towards creating a thriving and productive permaculture landscape.

Mulching: Mulching is the process of covering the soil surface with organic materials such as straw, leaves, wood chips, or even cardboard. This layer of mulch serves multiple purposes: it helps retain moisture, suppresses weed growth, regulates soil temperature, and gradually decomposes to add nutrients back into the soil. Additionally, mulching encourages the presence of beneficial organisms like earthworms, which aid in soil aeration and nutrient cycling.

Composting: Composting is the controlled decomposition of organic matter, resulting in a nutrient-rich, humus-like substance called compost. Adding compost to your garden provides your plants with essential nutrients and improves soil structure. Composting also helps recycle kitchen scraps and garden waste, reducing the amount of waste sent to landfills.

Cover cropping: Cover crops are plants grown specifically to improve soil health and fertility. They are typically fast-growing and can be easily incorporated into the soil after they have served their purpose. Some common cover crops include legumes (such as clover and beans), grasses (like rye and oats), and brassicas (like mustard and radish). Cover crops help prevent soil erosion, suppress weeds, and increase organic matter content. Legume cover crops also have the added benefit of fixing nitrogen from the atmosphere, making it available for other plants to use.

No-till or low-till gardening: Traditional tilling methods can disrupt soil structure, harm beneficial organisms, and contribute to soil erosion. No-till or low-till gardening involves minimal soil disturbance, allowing it to maintain its structure and supporting a healthy ecosystem of microorganisms. This can be achieved using techniques such as sheet mulching, lasagna gardening, or simply planting directly into the soil without turning it over.

Crop rotation: Crop rotation is the practice of growing different types of plants in the same area over a series of seasons. This helps prevent the buildup of pests and diseases, as well as the depletion of specific nutrients in the soil. By rotating crops, you can ensure that your soil remains balanced and fertile, giving your plants the nutrients they need to thrive.

Plant diversity: Incorporating a wide variety of plants in your permaculture garden not only creates a visually appealing landscape but also contributes to soil health. Different plants have varying root depths and nutrient requirements, which can help maintain a balanced soil ecosystem. Additionally, diverse plantings attract a range of beneficial insects and pollinators, further supporting the overall health of your garden.

In conclusion, natural soil regeneration techniques are essential for a successful permaculture garden. By implementing these practices, you will be nurturing a healthy, fertile, and sustainable soil ecosystem that will support the growth and productivity of your plants for years to come.

Implementing Permaculture Practices for Soil Health

In this section, we will delve into the practical implementation of permaculture practices that can significantly improve soil health. By incorporating these techniques into your garden or farm, you will create a sustainable and thriving ecosystem that supports plant and animal life. Let's explore some of the most effective permaculture practices for soil health.

No-Till Gardening: One of the core principles of permaculture is to work with nature, not against it. Traditional agricultural practices often involve tilling the soil, which disrupts the natural structure and balance of the soil ecosystem. No-till gardening is a permaculture practice that involves planting directly into the soil without turning it over. This helps maintain the soil's structure, preserves beneficial microorganisms, and reduces erosion.

Mulching: Mulching is the practice of covering the soil surface with organic materials such as leaves, straw, or wood chips. This serves multiple purposes: it helps retain moisture, suppresses weed growth, and provides a habitat for beneficial organisms. As the mulch breaks down, it also adds valuable nutrients back into the soil, improving its fertility and structure.

Composting: Composting is the process of decomposing organic matter into a nutrient-rich, soil-like material called humus. Adding compost to your garden provides your plants with essential nutrients and improves the overall soil structure. Composting also helps to reduce waste, as it repurposes kitchen scraps and yard waste that would otherwise end up in a landfill.

Plant Diversity: A diverse range of plant species is essential for a healthy permaculture garden. Different plants have varying root structures and nutrient requirements, which can help improve soil structure and nutrient cycling. Additionally, a diverse garden is more resilient to pests and diseases, reducing the need for chemical interventions.

Crop Rotation: Crop rotation is the practice of growing different types of crops in the same area over a series of seasons. This helps to prevent the buildup of pests and diseases that can occur when the same crop is grown repeatedly in the exact location. Crop rotation also helps to maintain soil fertility, as different plants have different nutrient requirements and can help balance the soil's nutrient levels.

Cover Crops: Cover crops are plants that are grown primarily to improve soil health rather than for harvest. They can be used to protect the soil from erosion, suppress weeds, and add organic matter to the soil. Some cover crops, such as legumes, can also fix nitrogen from the atmosphere, improving soil fertility.

Planting Perennials: Perennial plants are those that live for more than two years, and they play a vital role in permaculture gardens. Their deep root systems help to improve soil structure and reduce erosion. Additionally, perennials require less maintenance than annuals, as they do not need to be replanted each year.

By implementing these permaculture practices in your garden or farm, you will be well on your way to creating a healthy, regenerative soil ecosystem. In the next section, we will discuss monitoring and maintaining soil health in your permaculture garden to ensure its long-term success.

Monitoring and Maintaining Soil Health in Your Permaculture Garden

A thriving permaculture garden is a testament to the harmony between nature and human intervention. One of the critical aspects of this symbiosis is the health of the soil that supports the entire ecosystem. Monitoring and maintaining soil health is an **ongoing process.** It requires a keen understanding of the soil's needs and the ability to adapt to its ever-changing conditions. In this section, we will explore the various ways you can monitor and maintain the health of your permaculture garden's soil.

To begin with, it is essential to establish a baseline for your soil's health. This can be done by conducting a soil test, which will provide valuable information about the soil's pH, nutrient levels, and organic matter content. Soil tests can be done using at-home testing kits or by sending a sample to a professional laboratory. By understanding your soil's current state, you can make informed decisions about improving and maintaining its health.

Once you have established your soil's baseline, it is crucial to monitor its health regularly. This can be done through visual inspections, where you look for signs of healthy soil, such as the presence of earthworms, a crumbly texture, and a rich, earthy smell. Additionally, you can perform periodic soil tests to track changes in nutrient levels and pH over time.

One of the critical aspects of maintaining soil health in a permaculture garden is ensuring that the soil remains well-aerated and has proper drainage. Compacted soil can lead to poor root growth and reduced nutrient uptake by plants. To prevent soil compaction, avoid walking on your garden beds and use mulch to create pathways. You can also use tools like broad forks to gently aerate the soil without disrupting its structure.

Another essential aspect of soil health is maintaining a balance of nutrients. In a permaculture garden, this is often achieved through the use of organic matter, such as compost, manure, and mulch. These materials not only provide essential nutrients for plant growth but also help to improve the soil's structure and water retention capabilities. Regularly adding organic matter to your garden beds will **ensure your soil remains fertile** and productive.

In addition to organic matter, cover crops can play a vital role in maintaining soil health. Cover crops, such as clover, vetch, and rye, help to prevent soil erosion, suppress weeds, and fix nitrogen in the soil. By incorporating cover crops into your garden's rotation, you can ensure that your soil remains healthy and nutrient-rich.

Lastly, it is essential to practice crop rotation in your permaculture garden. By rotating the types of plants grown in a specific area, you can help prevent the buildup of pests and diseases while ensuring that the soil's nutrients are not depleted. A well-planned crop rotation will contribute to the overall health and productivity of your garden's soil.

In conclusion, monitoring and maintaining soil health is vital to successful permaculture gardening. By understanding your soil's needs and implementing practices such as proper aeration, organic matter addition, cover cropping, and crop rotation, you can ensure that your garden's soil remains healthy and productive for years to come. Remember, healthy soil is the foundation of a thriving permaculture garden. Your efforts in nurturing it will be rewarded with **bountiful harvests** and a flourishing ecosystem.

The Lasting Impact of Healthy Soil on Permaculture

In conclusion, the vitality and sustainability of any permaculture system are deeply rooted in the health of its soil. As we have explored throughout this chapter, understanding and nurturing soil composition is of paramount importance for the long-term success of your permaculture garden. By implementing the soil health and regeneration techniques discussed, you will not only witness a thriving ecosystem but also contribute to the global movement toward sustainable agriculture and environmental preservation.

The lasting impact of healthy soil on permaculture is multifaceted, as it not only supports the growth of diverse and resilient plant life but also fosters a balanced ecosystem teeming with beneficial microorganisms and insects. This, in turn, leads to increased productivity, reduced need for external inputs, and a more self-sufficient garden that can withstand the test of time.

Moreover, the principles of permaculture extend beyond the confines of your garden, as they encourage a shift in mindset towards a more holistic and interconnected view of the world around us. By nurturing the soil beneath our feet, we also nurture our communities, our planet, and ourselves. The regeneration of soil health is not just a means to an end but a journey of discovery and connection with the natural world.

As you continue on your permaculture journey, remember that soil health is an ongoing process that requires consistent care and attention. Regularly monitoring and maintaining your soil's health will ensure that it remains a fertile and productive foundation for your permaculture garden for years to come. Embrace the challenges and rewards of this responsibility, and take pride in the knowledge that your efforts contribute to a greener, more sustainable future for all.

In the words of the renowned environmentalist and permaculture pioneer, *Bill Mollison*, *"Permaculture is a philosophy of working with, rather than against nature; of protracted and thoughtful observation rather than protracted and thoughtless labor; and of looking at plants and animals in all their functions, rather than treating any area as a single project system."*

By prioritizing soil health and regeneration, you embody this philosophy and play a vital role in the global movement towards a more sustainable and harmonious existence with the natural world.

Chapter Summary

- Soil health is the foundation of a thriving permaculture ecosystem, playing a critical role in maintaining the balance of life on Earth.
- Soil is a complex, living ecosystem consisting of organic matter, minerals, water, air, and microorganisms, all of which contribute to plant growth and overall environmental health.
- Conventional agricultural practices have led to widespread soil degradation, making it essential to adopt permaculture techniques that prioritize soil health and regeneration.
- Natural soil regeneration techniques, such as mulching, composting, cover cropping, no-till gardening, crop rotation, and plant diversity, can significantly improve soil health and contribute to a sustainable garden ecosystem.
- Permaculture practices, including no-till gardening, mulching, composting, plant diversity, crop rotation, cover crops, and planting perennials, can help maintain and improve soil health.
- Monitoring and maintaining soil health is an ongoing process that involves regular visual inspections, soil testing, proper aeration, organic matter addition, cover cropping, and crop rotation.
- Healthy soil has a lasting impact on permaculture, supporting diverse and resilient plant life, fostering a balanced ecosystem, and contributing to the global movement toward sustainable agriculture and environmental preservation.
- Embracing the principles of permaculture and prioritizing soil health is essential for creating a greener, more sustainable future for all.

4

WATER MANAGEMENT AND CONSERVATION

A futuristic city with advanced water management systems, including rainwater harvesting skyscrapers, underground water storage facilities, and smart irrigation networks in urban gardens.

In the realm of permaculture, water is a vital and indispensable resource that plays a crucial role in the overall health and productivity of an ecosystem. As a finite resource, it is essential to manage and conserve water effectively to ensure the sustainability and resilience of our gardens, farms, and communities. This chapter will delve into the various aspects of water management and conservation in permaculture, providing practical solutions and techniques that can be applied to any landscape or environment.

As a holistic design system, permaculture emphasizes the importance of working with nature and its patterns rather than against it. This principle is particularly relevant when it comes to water management and conservation, as the natural water cycle is a perfect example of a closed-loop system that efficiently distributes and recycles water. By understanding and mimicking these natural processes, we can create regenerative and resilient systems that not only conserve water but also enhance the overall health of the ecosystem.

Water management and conservation in permaculture involve a multifaceted approach that includes harvesting rainwater, designing efficient irrigation systems, implementing greywater and rainwater systems, and employing strategies to reduce water waste and evaporation. By integrating these techniques into our permaculture designs, we can create landscapes that are not only productive and beautiful but also water-wise and sustainable.

In the following sections, we will explore the importance of water harvesting techniques and how they can be implemented in various settings. We will also discuss the design and implementation of efficient irrigation systems that minimize water waste and maximize productivity. Additionally, we will delve into the world of greywater and rainwater systems, providing practical solutions for capturing and reusing water in our homes and gardens.

Finally, we will examine strategies for reducing water waste and evaporation, ensuring that every drop of water is used effectively and responsibly.

As we navigate through this chapter, it is important to remember that

water is a precious resource that connects all living beings on our planet. By adopting responsible water management and conservation practices in our permaculture designs, we are not only contributing to the health and vitality of our ecosystems but also playing a vital role in the global effort to preserve and protect our planet's most valuable resource.

The Importance of Water Harvesting Techniques

In the realm of permaculture, water is undeniably one of the most vital resources for sustaining life and promoting the growth of plants, animals, and microorganisms. As a result, it is crucial for practitioners to develop and implement effective water harvesting techniques that not only ensure an adequate supply of water but also contribute to the overall health and sustainability of the ecosystem. This section will delve into the importance of water harvesting techniques and their role in fostering a thriving permaculture landscape.

Water harvesting techniques are essential for several reasons. Firstly, they help capture and store water from various sources such as rainfall, runoff, and underground springs. By doing so, these techniques provide a reliable and consistent water supply for plants and animals, even during drought or water scarcity. This is particularly important in arid and semi-arid regions, where water is often a limiting factor for the success of permaculture systems.

Secondly, water harvesting techniques are crucial in preventing soil erosion and nutrient loss. When water is allowed to flow freely across the landscape, it can carry away valuable topsoil and essential nutrients, leaving behind a degraded and less fertile environment. By capturing and directing water through carefully designed systems, permaculture practitioners can **minimize erosion** and ensure nutrients are retained within the ecosystem.

Moreover, water harvesting techniques contribute to the overall health and resilience of the permaculture system by promoting biodiversity and supporting the growth of various plant and animal species. For instance, creating swales, ponds, and other water features can provide a habitat for aquatic plants and animals and create microclimates that support a diverse range of species. This, in turn, leads to a more robust and adaptable ecosystem that can better withstand external pressures such as climate change and invasive species.

Additionally, water harvesting techniques can reduce the reliance on external water sources, such as municipal water supplies or groundwater extraction. By capturing and utilizing water on-site, permaculture practitioners can minimize their environmental footprint and contribute to conserving valuable water resources. This is particularly important in areas where water scarcity is a growing concern, as it helps to promote a more sustainable and self-sufficient approach to water management.

In conclusion, water harvesting techniques are indispensable to any successful permaculture system. By capturing, storing, and distributing water efficiently and sustainably, these techniques ensure the availability of this precious resource and contribute to the ecosystem's overall health, resilience, and sustainability. As we continue to face the challenges of climate change and increasing water scarcity, the importance of effective water harvesting techniques in permaculture cannot be overstated.

Designing Efficient Irrigation Systems

Designing efficient irrigation systems is crucial for water management and conservation in permaculture. With the right approach, you can ensure that your plants receive the optimal amount of water while minimizing waste and preserving this precious resource. In this section, we will explore the fundamental principles of designing efficient irrigation systems and discuss some of the most popular techniques used by permaculture practitioners around the world.

The first step in designing an efficient irrigation system is to understand the specific needs of your plants and the characteristics of your site. Different plants have varying water requirements, and factors such as soil type, climate, and topography can significantly impact the effectiveness of your irrigation system. By conducting a thorough site analysis and researching the water needs of your plants, you can tailor your irrigation system to suit the unique conditions of your permaculture garden.

One of the core principles of efficient irrigation is to deliver water directly to the root zone of your plants. This minimizes evaporation and runoff, ensuring your plants absorb the water you provide. **Drip irrigation**, also known as trickle irrigation, is a popular method that achieves this goal. In a drip irrigation system, water is slowly released through a network of tubes and emitters, allowing it to seep directly into the soil around the roots of your plants. This method is highly efficient, as it minimizes water waste and reduces the risk of overwatering.

Another effective irrigation technique is the use of **swales**, which are shallow-level trenches dug along the contour lines of your landscape. Swales help capture and slow the water flow, allowing it to infiltrate the soil and provide moisture to your plants. By strategically placing swales throughout your permaculture site, you can create a passive irrigation system that makes the most of the natural water movement across your land.

In addition to choosing a suitable irrigation method, it's essential to consider the timing and frequency of your watering. Watering your plants early in the morning or late in the evening can help to reduce evaporation, as the temperatures are cooler and the sun is less intense. Additionally, it's important to monitor the moisture levels in your soil and adjust your watering schedule accordingly. Overwatering can be as detrimental to your plants as underwatering, so finding the right balance for your site is crucial.

Finally, **mulching** is an excellent strategy for improving the efficiency of your irrigation system. By covering the soil around your plants with a layer of organic material, such as straw, leaves, or wood chips, you can help to retain moisture, regulate soil temperature, and reduce evaporation. Mulching also has the added benefit of suppressing weeds and adding nutrients to the soil as it breaks down over time.

In conclusion, designing efficient irrigation systems is essential to water management and conservation in permaculture. By understanding the needs of your plants and the characteristics of your site, selecting appropriate irrigation methods, and implementing strategies to reduce water waste and evaporation, you can create a sustainable and productive permaculture garden that thrives with minimal input. As water scarcity becomes an increasingly pressing global issue, the importance of efficient irrigation systems in permaculture will only continue to grow.

Implementing Greywater and Rainwater Systems

In the quest for sustainable living and efficient water management, greywater and rainwater systems have emerged as vital components of permaculture practices. These systems help conserve water and contribute to the overall health of your garden and the environment. In this section, we will delve into the benefits of these systems and provide practical guidance on how to implement them in your permaculture design.

Greywater refers to the gently used water from sinks, showers, and washing machines that can be reused for irrigation purposes. Recycling this water can significantly reduce your reliance on freshwater sources and lower your water bills. Rainwater, however, is a **free and abundant resource** that can be harvested and stored for various uses, including irrigation and household use, when properly treated.

To implement a greywater system, you must first assess the quality and quantity of the water you generate. This will help you determine the most suitable plants for your garden and the necessary filtration methods. It is essential to avoid using water contaminated with harsh chemicals, as it can harm your plants and the soil. Opt for eco-friendly cleaning products and consider installing a simple filtration system, such as a mulch basin, to remove any remaining particles before the water reaches your plants.

Next, you will need to design a distribution system that evenly disperses the greywater throughout your garden. Drip irrigation and subsurface systems are ideal, as they deliver water directly to the plant roots and minimize evaporation. Be sure to check your local regulations, as some areas may have specific guidelines or restrictions on greywater use.

Rainwater harvesting, on the other hand, involves collecting and storing rainwater for later use. This can be achieved through various methods, such as installing gutters and downspouts on your roof, which direct the water into storage tanks or barrels. You can also create swales and rain gardens to capture and store rainwater directly in your landscape.

When designing your rainwater system, consider factors such as the size of your roof, the average rainfall in your area, and your water needs. This will help you determine the appropriate storage capacity and whether you need additional filtration or treatment systems. Keep in mind that stored rainwater can be used for more than just irrigation; with proper treatment, it can also be used for household purposes, such as flushing toilets or even drinking.

In conclusion, implementing greywater and rainwater systems in your permaculture design is an effective way to conserve water, reduce waste, and promote a healthier ecosystem. By thoughtfully planning and incorporating these systems into your landscape, you can create a more sustainable and self-sufficient environment that benefits both your garden and the planet.

Strategies for Reducing Water Waste and Evaporation

In the world of permaculture, water is a precious resource that must be used wisely and efficiently. As we've explored various water management techniques in this chapter, it's crucial to address strategies for reducing water waste and evaporation. By implementing these methods, you can ensure that your permaculture garden remains sustainable and productive while also minimizing your ecological footprint.

Proper **irrigation scheduling** is one of the most effective ways to reduce water waste. By watering your plants at the right time and in the right amounts, you can avoid overwatering and ensure that your plants receive the moisture they need without wasting water. To achieve this, monitor the moisture levels in your soil and adjust your irrigation schedule accordingly. Watering in the early morning or late evening can also help minimize evaporation, as the temperatures are more relaxed and the sun is less intense.

Mulching is another essential strategy for reducing water waste and evaporation. Covering the soil with a layer of organic material, such as straw, wood chips, or leaves, can help retain moisture, regulate soil temperature, and reduce evaporation. Mulch also helps suppress weeds, which compete with your plants for water and nutrients. Be sure to replenish your mulch regularly, as it will break down over time and contribute to the fertility of your soil.

Incorporating **shade** into your permaculture design can also help reduce water waste and evaporation. By planting taller plants or trees to shade smaller plants, you can create a microclimate that helps retain moisture and reduces the need for frequent watering. Additionally, consider using shade cloth or other materials to protect your plants from the intense sun during the hottest parts of the day.

Another strategy for reducing water waste is to select **drought-tolerant plants** for your permaculture garden. These plants have adapted to thrive in low-water conditions. As a result, they can help you conserve water while enjoying a productive and diverse garden. Some examples of drought-tolerant plants include lavender, rosemary, sage, and various succulents. Be sure to research the specific water requirements of each plant to ensure that you provide the appropriate amount of moisture for their needs.

Lastly, proper **garden maintenance** can also help reduce water waste and evaporation. Regularly pruning your plants promotes healthy growth and reduces the amount of water they require. Additionally, keeping your garden free of weeds and pests can help ensure that your plants receive the water they need without competition from unwanted invaders.

In conclusion, implementing these strategies for reducing water waste and evaporation can help you create a more sustainable and efficient permaculture garden. By carefully managing your water resources and making thoughtful choices in your garden design, you can contribute to a healthier planet and enjoy the many benefits of a thriving permaculture ecosystem.

The Future of Water Conservation in Permaculture

As we reach the end of our exploration into water management and conservation in permaculture, it is essential to consider the future of this vital aspect of sustainable living. With climate change and increasing water scarcity becoming pressing global issues, efficient and environmentally friendly water management practices are more **crucial** than ever. Permaculture, with its emphasis on working in harmony with nature, offers a promising solution to these challenges.

In the coming years, we expect to see a greater focus on water conservation within the permaculture community. This will likely involve developing and refining innovative water harvesting techniques and the widespread adoption of efficient irrigation systems. In addition, as more people recognize the benefits of permaculture, we can anticipate a surge in the implementation of greywater and rainwater systems, which will not only conserve water but also reduce the strain on municipal water supplies.

Moreover, the future of water conservation in permaculture will likely involve a greater emphasis on education and awareness-raising. As more individuals understand the importance of water conservation and its role in creating a sustainable future, they will be more likely to adopt permaculture practices in their lives. This, in turn, will lead to a ripple effect as the benefits of water conservation become increasingly apparent on a larger scale.

Another critical aspect of the future of water conservation in permaculture is the ongoing development of strategies for reducing water waste and evaporation. This will involve not only the creation of new techniques but also the refinement of existing ones, ensuring that they are as effective as possible. By continually improving upon these strategies, permaculture practitioners will be better equipped to conserve water and create resilient ecosystems.

In conclusion, the future of water conservation in permaculture is bright, filled with innovation, collaboration, and a commitment to working in harmony with the natural world. By embracing permaculture principles and implementing effective water management practices, we can help create a more sustainable and resilient future for ourselves and future generations. As we continue to face the challenges of climate change and water scarcity, the importance of water conservation in permaculture will only continue to grow, making it an essential component of our efforts to build a better world.

Chapter Summary

- Water is a vital and indispensable resource in permaculture, playing a crucial role in the overall health and productivity of an ecosystem. Effective water management and conservation are essential for ensuring the sustainability and resilience of our gardens, farms, and communities.
- Water harvesting techniques are crucial for capturing and storing water from various sources, preventing soil erosion and nutrient loss, promoting biodiversity, and reducing reliance on external water sources.
- Designing efficient irrigation systems involves understanding the specific needs of plants and site characteristics, delivering water directly to the root zone, using methods such as drip irrigation and swales, and proper scheduling to minimize water waste and evaporation.
- Implementing greywater and rainwater systems can help conserve water, reduce waste, and promote a healthier ecosystem. Greywater systems recycle gently used water from sinks, showers, and washing machines for irrigation purposes, while rainwater systems collect and store rainwater for various uses.
- Reducing water waste and evaporation can be achieved through proper irrigation scheduling, mulching, incorporating shade into the garden design, selecting drought-tolerant plants, and maintaining the garden properly.
- The future of water conservation in permaculture will likely involve a greater focus on innovative water harvesting techniques, efficient irrigation systems, and widespread adoption of greywater and rainwater systems.

- Education and awareness-raising will play a significant role in the future of water conservation in permaculture as more individuals understand the importance of water conservation and adopt permaculture practices in their own lives.
- The ongoing development of strategies for reducing water waste and evaporation, as well as the refinement of existing techniques, will be crucial in ensuring effective water conservation and creating resilient ecosystems in permaculture.

5

PLANT SELECTION AND COMPANION PLANTING

An enchanting garden scene where a tall sunflower stands proudly among a group of low-growing, vibrant green basil plants, with ladybugs happily exploring the leaves, showcasing the beauty and benefits of companion planting.

Welcome to chapter 5, where we delve into the fascinating world of plant selection and companion planting in the context of practical permaculture. As a permaculture enthusiast, you are likely already aware of the importance of working with nature to create sustainable, resilient, and productive systems. One of the critical aspects of achieving this is through the **careful selection of plants** and the **strategic placement** of these plants in your garden. This chapter aims to provide you with the knowledge and tools necessary to make informed decisions about the plants you choose and how they interact, ultimately contributing to the success of your permaculture garden.

Plant selection and companion planting are interconnected concepts crucial to designing and implementing any permaculture system. Plant selection refers to the process of choosing the right plants for your garden based on various factors such as climate, soil type, water availability, and the specific needs of your garden ecosystem. On the other hand, companion planting is the art and science of arranging plants in close proximity to one another so that they can mutually benefit from each other's presence. This can include providing nutrients, attracting beneficial insects, repelling pests, or creating a more favorable microclimate.

In this chapter, we will explore the importance of plant diversity in permaculture and the various criteria you should consider when selecting plants for your garden. We will then delve into the world of companion planting, discussing its benefits and techniques and providing examples of successful plant combinations. Finally, we will conclude with a discussion on how to maximize the potential of your permaculture garden through thoughtful plant selection and companion planting.

By the end of this chapter, you will have a deeper understanding of the principles and practices of plant selection and companion planting, empowering you to make informed decisions that will enhance the productivity, resilience, and sustainability of your permaculture garden. So, let's embark on this exciting journey together and discover the incredible potential that lies within the world of plants!

Understanding the Importance of Plant Diversity in Permaculture

Plant diversity is a fundamental principle of permaculture, and for a good reason. In this section, we will delve into the importance of plant diversity in permaculture, exploring its numerous benefits and how it contributes to a thriving, resilient, and sustainable garden ecosystem.

At the heart of permaculture is the concept of working with nature rather than against it. By embracing plant diversity, we are **mimicking the natural ecosystems** that have evolved over millions of years. In nature, a diverse range of plant species coexist, each fulfilling a specific role and contributing to the overall health and stability of the ecosystem. By incorporating a wide variety of plants in our permaculture gardens, we can harness the power of nature's wisdom and create a more resilient, productive, and sustainable system.

Key Benefits to Promoting Plant Diversity in Permaculture

Improved Soil Health: Different plants have varying root structures and nutrient requirements, which can help to improve soil structure and fertility. For example, deep-rooted plants can break up compacted soil and bring nutrients up to the surface, while nitrogen-fixing plants can replenish essential nutrients in the soil.

Pest and Disease Control: A diverse garden is less susceptible to pest and disease outbreaks, as it is more difficult for a single pest or pathogen to spread rapidly through a varied plant population. Additionally, many plants have natural pest-repelling properties and can be strategically placed to protect more vulnerable species.

Pollinator Attraction: A diverse range of flowering plants will attract a wide variety of pollinators, essential for reproducing many fruit and vegetable crops. This not only increases the productivity of your garden but also supports local biodiversity and the overall health of the ecosystem.

Climate Resilience: By incorporating plants with varying tolerances to temperature, moisture, and other environmental factors, you can create a garden that is more resilient to the impacts of climate change and extreme weather events.

Enhanced Productivity: Plant diversity can increase productivity, as different plants can be harvested at different times, ensuring a continuous supply of fresh produce throughout the growing season. Moreover, diverse gardens are more likely to include plants with multiple uses, such as those that provide food, medicine, or materials for building or crafting.

Aesthetics and Well-being: A diverse garden is not only functional but also beautiful and inspiring. Research has shown that spending time in natural environments with a high level of biodiversity can have significant mental health benefits, including reduced stress and increased well-being.

In conclusion, plant diversity is a cornerstone of permaculture, offering numerous benefits for both the garden and the gardener. By understanding and embracing the importance of plant diversity, we can create thriving, resilient, and sustainable permaculture systems that work in harmony with nature and provide abundant resources for ourselves and future generations.

Criteria for Choosing the Right Plants for Your Permaculture Garden

Selecting the right plants for your permaculture garden is crucial in ensuring its success. By carefully considering each plant's unique characteristics, you can create a productive and sustainable thriving ecosystem. This section will explore the critical criteria for choosing plants for your permaculture garden.

Climate and Hardiness

The first factor to consider when selecting plants is the climate in your garden. Choosing plants that are well-suited to the local climate is essential, as this will ensure their survival and growth. To do this, research the hardiness zones of various plants and select appropriate ones for your area. Hardiness zones are a classification system that indicates the minimum temperatures a plant can withstand.

Soil Type and Nutrient Requirements

Different plants have varying preferences for soil type and nutrient levels. Therefore, when selecting plants for your permaculture garden, it's important to consider the existing soil conditions and choose plants that will thrive in those conditions. Additionally, some plants can help improve soil quality by adding nutrients or breaking up compacted soil, so consider incorporating these into your garden design.

Sunlight and Water Needs

Just as plants have different soil preferences, they also have varying sunlight and water requirements. When choosing plants for your permaculture garden, consider the amount of sunlight and water that each plant will receive in its designated location. Select plants that are well-suited to the available resources, and arrange them in a way that maximizes their access to sunlight and water.

Size and Growth Habit

A plant's size and growth habits are essential factors to consider when designing your permaculture garden. Be sure to choose plants that will not outgrow their allotted space, as overcrowding can lead to competition for resources and reduced productivity. Additionally, consider the growth habits of each plant, such as whether they are climbers, groundcovers, or tall and upright, and arrange them in a way that maximizes their potential.

Edible and Medicinal Qualities

One of the primary goals of permaculture is to create a productive and self-sustaining ecosystem. To achieve this, it's essential to select plants that provide multiple functions, such as food and medicine. Therefore, when choosing plants for your permaculture garden, prioritize those that offer edible or medicinal benefits, as these will contribute to the overall productivity and resilience of your garden.

Pest and Disease Resistance

A healthy permaculture garden can withstand pests and diseases with minimal intervention. When selecting plants, prioritize those with natural pest and disease resistance. This will reduce the need for chemical treatments and help maintain a balanced ecosystem. Additionally, consider incorporating plants that attract beneficial insects, such as ladybugs and lacewings, which can help control pest populations.

Compatibility with Companion Plants

Finally, when choosing plants for your permaculture garden, consider their compatibility with other plants in the ecosystem. Companion planting is a technique that involves strategically placing plants together to maximize their mutual benefits, such as improved nutrient uptake, pest control, and pollination. You can create a harmonious and productive permaculture garden by selecting plants that work well together.

In conclusion, selecting the right plants for your permaculture garden involves careful consideration of various factors, including climate, soil type, sunlight and water needs, size and growth habits, edible and medicinal qualities, pest and disease resistance, and compatibility with companion plants. By keeping these criteria in mind, you can create a thriving and sustainable permaculture garden that meets your unique needs and goals.

The Art and Science of Companion Planting: Benefits and Techniques

Companion planting is a time-honored gardening technique practiced for centuries by farmers and gardeners alike. It is a method of growing different plants together so that they can mutually benefit from each other. This symbiotic relationship enhances the productivity and resilience of your permaculture garden and contributes to its overall health and sustainability. In this section, we will delve into the art and science of companion planting, exploring its benefits and techniques that can be applied to your permaculture garden.

The Benefits of Companion Planting

Companion planting offers a myriad of benefits for your permaculture garden. Some of the most notable advantages include the following:

Pest control: Certain plants can repel or attract insects, which can help keep pests in check without the need for harmful chemicals. For example, marigolds are known to deter nematodes, while basil can help ward off flies and mosquitoes.

Improved pollination: Planting flowers and herbs near your fruit and vegetable crops can attract pollinators such as bees and butterflies, which can improve the pollination and yield of your plants.

Enhanced nutrient availability: Some plants, like legumes, can fix nitrogen from the atmosphere and make it available to other plants. This can help improve soil fertility and reduce the need for synthetic fertilizers.

Natural support: Tall plants like sunflowers or corn can support climbing plants like beans and peas, reducing the need for artificial structures.

Improved soil structure: Planting deep-rooted plants alongside shallow-rooted ones can help break up compacted soil and improve its structure, allowing for better water infiltration and root growth.

The Techniques of Companion Planting

To successfully implement companion planting in your permaculture garden, consider the following techniques:

Research plant relationships: Before planting, take the time to research which plants grow well together and which ones may inhibit each other's growth. This will help you create a harmonious garden where plants can thrive and support one another.

Plan your garden layout: Design your garden in a way that takes advantage of the natural relationships between plants. For example, you can plant nitrogen-fixing legumes near nitrogen-hungry plants like tomatoes or corn or plant pest-repelling herbs near plants that are susceptible to pests.

Utilize plant guilds: Plant guilds are groups of plants that work well together and support each other's growth. For example, the *"Three Sisters"* guild consists of corn, beans, and squash, which provide support, nitrogen, and ground cover, respectively. Incorporating plant guilds into your permaculture garden can help create a balanced and productive ecosystem.

Rotate your crops: Rotating your crops each year can help prevent the buildup of pests and diseases in your garden. By changing the location of your plants, you can disrupt the life cycles of pests and reduce the likelihood of disease transmission.

Observe and adapt: As with any gardening technique, it's essential to observe your garden and make adjustments as needed. Pay attention to how your plants are growing and interacting with one another, and be prepared to change your companion planting strategy if necessary.

In conclusion, the art and science of companion planting can significantly enhance the productivity, health, and sustainability of your permaculture garden. By carefully selecting plants that complement one another and implementing thoughtful planting techniques, you can create a thriving ecosystem that maximizes the potential of your garden while minimizing the need for external inputs.

Maximizing the Potential of Your Permaculture Garden

In conclusion, the power to maximize the potential of your permaculture garden lies in the thoughtful and strategic implementation of plant selection and companion planting. When combined effectively, these two essential components can create a **thriving**, **sustainable**, and **productive ecosystem** that benefits the environment and enriches the lives of those who tend to it.

Throughout this chapter, we have explored the importance of plant diversity in permaculture and the various criteria to consider when choosing the right plants for your garden. By selecting plants well-suited to your climate, soil, and available resources, you can ensure that your garden remains resilient and adaptable to changing conditions.

We have also delved into the art and science of companion planting, highlighting the numerous benefits it offers, such as pest control, nutrient cycling, and improved pollination. By understanding the relationships between different plants and utilizing various companion planting techniques, you can create a harmonious and balanced garden that supports the growth and health of all its inhabitants.

As you embark on your permaculture adventure, remember that the key to success lies in observation, experimentation, and adaptation. By continually learning from your garden and adjusting your approach as needed, you can create a thriving ecosystem that not only provides for your needs but also contributes to the health and well-being of the planet.

In the end, the true beauty of permaculture lies in its ability to connect us with the natural world and remind us of our role as caretakers of the Earth. By embracing plant selection and companion planting, you are taking an important step towards creating a more sustainable, resilient, and abundant future for yourself and future generations.

Chapter Summary

- Plant selection and companion planting are essential components of permaculture, contributing to the success of a sustainable and productive garden ecosystem.
- Plant diversity is crucial in permaculture, as it promotes soil health, pest and disease control, pollinator attraction, climate resilience, enhanced productivity, and overall well-being.
- When selecting plants for a permaculture garden, consider factors such as climate, soil type, sunlight, water needs, size and growth habits, edible and medicinal qualities, pest and disease resistance, and compatibility with companion plants.

- Companion planting is the strategic arrangement of plants in close proximity to one another, allowing them to mutually benefit from each other's presence through improved nutrient uptake, pest control, and pollination.
- Benefits of companion planting include pest control, improved pollination, enhanced nutrient availability, natural support, and improved soil structure.
- Techniques for successful companion planting include researching plant relationships, planning the garden layout, utilizing plant guilds, rotating crops, and observing and adapting as needed.
- Maximizing the potential of a permaculture garden through plant selection and companion planting requires continuous observation, experimentation, and adaptation, ultimately contributing to a more sustainable, resilient, and abundant future.

6

CREATING DIVERSE AND RESILIENT ECOSYSTEMS

A lush tropical rainforest, highlighting the layers of the forest, from the canopy to the forest floor, and featuring a diverse array of flora and fauna interconnected within the ecosystem.

In the world of permaculture, the concepts of diversity and resilience are not just *buzzwords*; they are the very foundation of a thriving, sustainable ecosystem. As we face the challenges of climate change, habitat loss, and dwindling resources, it becomes increasingly important to create landscapes that can adapt and flourish in the face of adversity. In this chapter, we will explore the critical role that diverse and resilient ecosystems play in permaculture and how you can incorporate these principles into your own garden or farm.

At its core, permaculture is about **working with nature** rather than against it. This means observing and learning from the natural world and using that knowledge to design productive and self-sustaining systems. One of the key lessons we can learn from nature is the value of diversity. In a diverse ecosystem, a wide variety of plant and animal species coexist, each fulfilling a unique role and contributing to the overall health and stability of the system.

Diversity is important for several reasons. First, it provides a buffer against pests and diseases. When a single species dominates an ecosystem, it becomes vulnerable to outbreaks that can wipe out entire populations. By contrast, a diverse ecosystem is more resilient, as the presence of multiple species helps to keep pests and diseases in check.

Second, diversity promotes soil health and fertility. Different plants have different nutrient requirements and root structures, which can help to improve soil structure and prevent nutrient depletion. Finally, diversity supports a wide range of beneficial insects, birds, and other wildlife, which play crucial roles in pollination, pest control, and nutrient cycling.

Resilience is another crucial aspect of permaculture; it goes hand in hand with diversity. A resilient ecosystem can withstand disturbances like drought, floods, or temperature fluctuations and bounce back quickly. In a resilient system, the various components – plants, animals, and microorganisms – work together to maintain balance and stability, even in the face of change. This is particularly important in climate change, as we expect more frequent and severe weather events in the coming years.

In the following sections, we will delve deeper into the role of plant and animal species in building ecosystem diversity, discuss strategies for designing resilient permaculture systems, and explore how to integrate natural elements and processes into your garden or farm. So, let's embark on this exciting journey towards creating a more diverse and resilient world, one permaculture garden at a time!

The Role of Plant and Animal Species in Building Ecosystem Diversity

In the world of permaculture, diversity is critical to creating a thriving and resilient ecosystem. By incorporating a wide variety of plant and animal species, we can mimic the natural processes found in nature and promote a self-sustaining environment. In this section, we will delve into the importance of plant and animal species in building ecosystem diversity and how they contribute to the overall health and productivity of a permaculture system.

The Benefits of Plant Diversity

Plant diversity plays a crucial role in the overall health and productivity of a permaculture system. By incorporating a wide range of plant species, we can achieve several benefits:

Improved Soil Health: Different plants contribute to soil health in various ways. Some plants, such as legumes, fix nitrogen in the soil, while others, like deep-rooted plants, help break up compacted soil and improve aeration. This diverse array of plants helps create rich and fertile soil that supports the growth of other species.

Pest and Disease Control: A diverse plant community can help reduce the risk of pest and disease outbreaks. A single species dominating an area can create a monoculture more susceptible to pests and diseases. By incorporating a variety of plants, we can disrupt the life cycles of pests and diseases, making it more difficult for them to establish and spread.

Pollinator Attraction: A diverse array of flowering plants can attract a wide range of pollinators, such as bees, butterflies, and birds. These pollinators are essential for the reproduction of many plant species. They can increase the overall productivity of your permaculture system.

The Importance of Animal Species in Ecosystem Diversity

In addition to plant diversity, incorporating various animal species into your permaculture system can contribute to **ecosystem diversity.** Animals play several essential roles in a permaculture system, including:

Nutrient Cycling: Animals help cycle nutrients through the ecosystem by consuming plants and other organisms, breaking them down, and depositing their waste into the soil. This process helps maintain soil fertility and supports plant growth.

Pest Control: Many animal species, such as birds and insects, can help control pest populations by feeding on them. By encouraging a diverse range of animal species in your permaculture system, you can create a natural form of pest control that reduces the need for chemical interventions.

Pollination: As mentioned earlier, pollinators play a crucial role in plant reproduction. By incorporating animal species that act as pollinators, you can support the growth and productivity of your permaculture system.

Habitat Creation: By providing diverse habitats for various animal species, you can support a thriving ecosystem that contributes to the overall health and resilience of your permaculture system.

In conclusion, the role of plant and animal species in building ecosystem diversity is essential for the success of any permaculture system. By incorporating a wide range of species, we can create a self-sustaining environment resilient to pests, diseases, and environmental changes. The following sections will explore strategies for designing resilient permaculture systems and integrating natural elements and processes to further enhance ecosystem diversity.

Designing for Resilience: Strategies for Adapting to Environmental Changes

In a world where climate change and environmental degradation are increasingly affecting our ecosystems, designing resilient permaculture systems is more important than ever. By incorporating strategies that enable adaptation to environmental changes, we can create landscapes that withstand disturbances and thrive in adversity. This section will explore various strategies for designing resilient permaculture systems that adapt to various environmental changes.

Embrace diversity: One of the most effective ways to build resilience is by incorporating a diverse range of plant and animal species into your permaculture system. This diversity helps to create a more stable ecosystem, as different species can fill various ecological niches and provide a wide range of functions. In addition, in the event of a disturbance, such as a disease outbreak or pest infestation, a diverse ecosystem is more likely to recover quickly and maintain its overall health.

Utilize polycultures: Polycultures, or the practice of growing multiple species together, can help to increase the resilience of your permaculture system. By interplanting different species, you can create a more complex and interconnected ecosystem that is better able to withstand environmental changes. Polycultures can also help reduce the risk of disease and pest infestations, making it more difficult for pests to spread and establish themselves within the system.

Design for redundancy: Redundancy is critical in designing resilient systems. By incorporating multiple species that serve similar functions, you can ensure that your permaculture system continues functioning even if one species is lost or damaged. For example, planting several types of nitrogen-fixing plants can help to maintain soil fertility even if one species is affected by a disease or pest.

Foster soil health: Healthy soil is the foundation of a resilient permaculture system. By focusing on building and maintaining soil health, you can create an environment that supports a diverse range of plant and animal species. This can be achieved through composting, mulching, and using cover crops to protect and nourish the soil.

Plan for water management: Water is a critical resource for any permaculture system. Designing for resilience includes planning for both water abundance and scarcity. By incorporating strategies such as rainwater harvesting, swales, and drought-tolerant plant species, you can help ensure that your permaculture system remains productive and healthy even during water stress.

Encourage natural pest control: By creating a diverse and interconnected ecosystem, you can encourage natural predators to help control pest populations. This not only reduces the need for chemical interventions but also contributes to the overall resilience of your permaculture system. For example, planting a variety of flowering plants can help to attract beneficial insects while providing habitat for birds and other predators can help to keep pest populations in check.

By incorporating these strategies into your permaculture design, you can create a diverse and resilient ecosystem that can better adapt to environmental changes. As we face increasing challenges from climate change and other environmental pressures, designing for resilience is not only a practical approach but also a necessary one for the long-term success of our permaculture systems.

Integrating Natural Elements and Processes into Your Permaculture System

In order to create a thriving permaculture system, it is essential to integrate natural elements and processes into your design. By working with nature rather than against it, you can harness its power to create a more diverse and resilient ecosystem. This section will explore ways to incorporate natural elements and processes into your permaculture system, ultimately leading to a more sustainable and harmonious environment.

Observe and Mimic Nature

The first step in integrating natural elements and processes into your permaculture system is to carefully observe the natural world around you. By studying the patterns and relationships in nature, you can gain valuable insights into designing your own system. For example, you might notice how certain plants grow well together or how specific animals contribute to the health of an ecosystem. You can create a more diverse and resilient permaculture system by mimicking these natural relationships.

Utilize Natural Energy Sources

One of the fundamental principles of permaculture is using renewable resources and natural energy sources. This can include harnessing the power of the sun, wind, and water to provide energy for your system. By incorporating solar panels, wind turbines, or hydroelectric systems into your design, you can reduce your reliance on non-renewable energy sources and create a more sustainable ecosystem.

Encourage Natural Pest Control

Instead of relying on harmful chemicals to control pests, consider integrating natural pest control methods into your permaculture system. This can include introducing beneficial insects, such as ladybugs and lacewings, which prey on harmful pests. Additionally, planting certain species of plants can help deter pests, as their strong scents or natural toxins can repel unwanted insects. By encouraging natural pest control, you can reduce the need for harmful pesticides and create a healthier ecosystem.

Build Healthy Soil

Healthy soil is the foundation of any successful permaculture system. In order to create a diverse and resilient ecosystem, it is essential to focus on building and maintaining healthy soil. This can be achieved through various methods, such as composting, mulching, and no-till gardening. By nurturing the soil, you can support a diverse array of plant and animal life, ultimately leading to a more resilient ecosystem.

Incorporate Water Management Strategies

Water is a critical component of any permaculture system, and it is essential to manage it effectively. By integrating natural water management strategies, such as rainwater harvesting, swales, and greywater recycling, you can ensure that your system has a consistent and sustainable water supply. These methods not only help conserve water but also contribute to your ecosystem's overall health and resilience.

In conclusion, integrating natural elements and processes into your permaculture system is crucial for creating a diverse and resilient ecosystem. By observing and mimicking nature, utilizing natural energy sources, encouraging natural pest control, building healthy soil, and incorporating water management strategies, you can create a sustainable and harmonious environment that thrives in the face of environmental challenges.

The Lasting Impact of Embracing Diversity and Resilience in Permaculture

In conclusion, the journey towards creating diverse and resilient ecosystems in permaculture is not only a rewarding endeavor but also a crucial step in ensuring the long-term sustainability and success of our agricultural systems. By embracing the principles of diversity and resilience, we can cultivate landscapes that are more adaptable to environmental changes, more productive, and more beneficial to both humans and the natural world.

The importance of fostering diversity in permaculture cannot be overstated. Incorporating various plant and animal species into our systems can create a more balanced and harmonious ecosystem that is less susceptible to pests, diseases, and other threats. This diversity also provides a wealth of resources for humans, from nutritious food to valuable materials and medicines.

Resilience, on the other hand, is the ability of an ecosystem to adapt and thrive in the face of change. By designing our permaculture systems with resilience in mind, we can ensure they will continue flourishing even as the climate and other environmental factors shift. This adaptability is essential for the survival of our agricultural systems and the well-being of the communities that rely on them.

Integrating natural elements and processes into our permaculture systems is another critical aspect of building diverse and resilient ecosystems. By working with nature rather than against it, we can create systems that are more in tune with the natural world and better equipped to handle the challenges that come their way.

As we move forward in our quest to create more sustainable and regenerative agricultural systems, let us remember the importance of embracing diversity and resilience in our permaculture designs. By doing so, we can ensure that our landscapes not only provide for our needs but also contribute to the health and well-being of the planet as a whole. In the end, the lasting impact of diverse and resilient permaculture ecosystems will be felt not only by those who practice it but also by future generations who will inherit a more sustainable and vibrant world.

Chapter Summary

- Diversity and resilience are foundational principles in permaculture, essential for creating sustainable and adaptable ecosystems that can withstand challenges such as climate change, habitat loss, and dwindling resources.
- Plant and animal species are crucial in building ecosystem diversity, contributing to improved soil health, pest and disease control, pollinator attraction, nutrient cycling, and habitat creation.
- Designing for resilience involves embracing diversity, utilizing polycultures, designing for redundancy, fostering soil health, and planning for water management to create ecosystems that can adapt to environmental changes.
- Integrating natural elements and processes, such as observing and mimicking nature, utilizing natural energy sources, encouraging natural pest control, building healthy soil, and

incorporating water management strategies, is essential for creating a diverse and resilient permaculture system.

- Embracing diversity in permaculture leads to more balanced and harmonious ecosystems, providing a wealth of resources for humans and reducing susceptibility to pests, diseases, and other threats.
- Resilience in permaculture ensures that ecosystems can adapt and thrive in the face of change, which is essential for the survival of agricultural systems and the well-being of communities that rely on them.
- Prioritizing diversity and resilience in permaculture designs contributes to the health and well-being of the planet, creating a lasting impact that will benefit both current practitioners and future generations.

7

INTEGRATING LIVESTOCK AND WILDLIFE

A whimsical farm scene where livestock and wildlife animals are having a friendly picnic together, with cows, deer, pigs, rabbits, and birds sharing food and enjoying each other's company under a large, shady tree.

In the world of permaculture, the integration of livestock and wildlife is a vital component in creating a thriving, sustainable ecosystem. This harmonious relationship between domesticated animals and their wild counterparts is not only fascinating but also essential for the long-term success of any permaculture system. By understanding and nurturing this symbiotic relationship, we can cultivate a productive and resilient environment that benefits all living beings within it.

At the heart of permaculture lies the principle of **working with nature** rather than against it. This means recognizing the inherent value of every living organism and the role it plays in the ecosystem. Livestock and wildlife are no exception. By integrating these two elements, we can tap into their unique strengths and abilities, creating a balanced and diverse landscape that supports a wide range of species.

Livestock can provide numerous benefits to a permaculture system, such as producing food, improving soil fertility, and controlling pests. At the same time, wildlife contributes to the overall health of the ecosystem by pollinating plants, dispersing seeds, and maintaining a balance of predator and prey populations. When these two groups coexist and interact, they form a mutually beneficial relationship that enhances the overall productivity and resilience of the permaculture system.

This chapter will explore how livestock and wildlife can be integrated into a permaculture design, from choosing the right animals for your system to creating habitats that encourage wildlife to thrive. We will also discuss how to manage interactions between livestock and wildlife to ensure that both groups benefit from their coexistence and address potential challenges and conflicts that may arise.

By understanding the symbiotic relationship between livestock and wildlife, we can create a permaculture system that not only produces food and resources for human consumption but also supports a diverse and thriving ecosystem. This holistic approach to land management is the key to building a sustainable future for ourselves and the countless species with whom we share this planet.

Choosing the Right Livestock for Your Permaculture System

Selecting the appropriate livestock for your permaculture system ensures a harmonious and productive integration of animals and plants. The right livestock can provide numerous benefits, such as nutrient cycling, pest control, and food production. This section will discuss the factors to consider when choosing livestock and offer some examples of animals that can be successfully incorporated into a permaculture system.

Assessing Your Needs and Goals: Before diving into the world of livestock, it's essential to assess your specific needs and goals for your permaculture system. Are you looking to produce food for your family, or are you more focused on creating a sustainable ecosystem? Your objectives will help guide your decision-making when selecting the right animals for your system.

Climate and Environment: The climate and environment of your permaculture site play a significant role in determining which livestock will thrive. Some animals are better suited to colder climates, while others prefer warmer temperatures. Additionally, the availability of water, vegetation, and shelter will impact the types of animals that can be successfully integrated into your system.

Size and Space Requirements: The size of your permaculture site and the space available for livestock will also influence your choices. Smaller animals, such as chickens and rabbits, require less space and can be easily accommodated in most permaculture systems. However, larger animals, like cows and goats, need more room to roam and graze, so it's essential to ensure that you have adequate space to meet their needs.

Skills and Experience: Your level of experience and comfort with handling livestock should also be considered when selecting animals for your permaculture system. If you are new to raising livestock, it's wise to start with low-maintenance animals, such as chickens or ducks, before moving on to more challenging species.

Examples of Livestock for Permaculture Systems

Here are some examples of livestock that can be successfully integrated into a permaculture system:

- **Chickens**: These versatile birds provide eggs, meat, and natural pest control. They can also help with composting by turning and aerating the soil.
- **Ducks:** Ducks are excellent foragers and can help control pests like slugs and snails. They also produce eggs and meat.
- **Goats:** These hardy animals can provide milk, meat, and fiber, while also helping to control weeds and brush.
- **Sheep:** Sheep can offer meat, wool, and milk, and they are efficient grazers that can help maintain pasture health.
- **Pigs:** Pigs are natural rototillers, turning over soil and helping to break up compacted ground. They can also provide meat and help with composting.
- **Bees:** These essential pollinators can increase your garden's productivity and provide honey.

In conclusion, choosing the right livestock for your permaculture system involves considering your needs, goals, climate, available space, and experience. By carefully selecting the appropriate animals, you can create a thriving ecosystem that benefits both livestock and wildlife.

Creating Habitats for Wildlife to Thrive

In a thriving permaculture system, wildlife plays a crucial role in maintaining balance and harmony. By creating habitats that cater to the needs of various species, you can encourage a diverse range of wildlife to flourish alongside your livestock. This section will explore the different ways you can create and enhance habitats for wildlife to thrive in your permaculture system.

First and foremost, it's essential to understand the specific needs of the wildlife species you wish to attract. Each species has unique requirements for food, water, shelter, and breeding sites. Providing these essentials allows you to create a welcoming environment that encourages wildlife to make your permaculture system their home.

One effective way to create habitats for wildlife is by planting a diverse range of **native plants**. Native plants are well-adapted to the local climate and soil conditions, making them a perfect choice for supporting local wildlife. These plants provide food, shelter, and nesting sites for various species, including pollinators, birds, and small mammals. Additionally, native plants often require less maintenance and water, making them a sustainable choice for your permaculture system.

Water sources are another critical component of wildlife habitats. By incorporating ponds, streams, or even small birdbaths into your permaculture design, you can attract a variety of species that depend on water for survival. Ensure that water sources are clean and accessible. Consider adding rocks or logs to provide additional shelter and basking spots for amphibians and reptiles.

Another essential aspect of creating habitats for wildlife to thrive is **shelter**. Providing a variety of shelter options, such as brush piles, rock piles, and nesting boxes, can accommodate the needs of different species. These shelters offer protection from predators and harsh weather conditions, as well as nesting and breeding sites.

In addition to providing food, water, and shelter, it's crucial to consider the connectivity of your permaculture system. Wildlife corridors like hedgerows and tree lines allow animals to move safely between different habitats. These corridors are essential for maintaining genetic diversity and ensuring the long-term survival of various species.

Finally, practicing responsible **land management** is essential to create habitats for wildlife to thrive. This includes minimizing the use of pesticides and herbicides, which can harm wildlife and your livestock. Instead, opt for natural pest control methods, such as introducing beneficial insects and practicing crop rotation.

In conclusion, creating habitats for wildlife to thrive is an integral part of a successful permaculture system. By providing food, water, shelter, and connectivity essentials, you can encourage diverse species to coexist harmoniously with your livestock. This benefits the wildlife and contributes to the overall health and productivity of your permaculture system.

Managing Livestock and Wildlife Interactions for Mutual Benefit

In a well-designed permaculture system, livestock and wildlife can coexist harmoniously, each benefiting from the presence of the other. This section will explore various strategies for managing livestock and wildlife interactions to ensure a mutually beneficial relationship.

Encouraging Natural Pest Control

One of the primary benefits of integrating livestock and wildlife in a permaculture system is the natural pest control that can be achieved. Many wild animals, such as birds, frogs, and insects, feed on common pests that can damage crops and harm livestock. Creating habitats that attract these beneficial creatures can reduce the need for chemical pesticides and promote a healthier ecosystem.

To **encourage natural pest control**, consider the following strategies:

- Plant a variety of native plants that provide food and shelter for beneficial insects and birds.
- Install birdhouses, bat boxes, and other nesting sites to attract insect-eating species.
- Create small ponds or wetland areas to support amphibians and other aquatic wildlife.
- Avoid using chemical pesticides, which can harm beneficial species as well as pests.

Grazing Management for Soil Health

Grazing livestock, such as cows, sheep, and goats, can be crucial in maintaining soil health and fertility. Their grazing habits help to control weeds, aerate the soil, and recycle nutrients through their manure.

However, it's essential to manage grazing patterns to prevent overgrazing and soil compaction.

Rotational grazing is an effective strategy for managing livestock and promoting soil health. This involves dividing your land into smaller paddocks and moving your livestock between them on a regular basis. This allows the vegetation in each paddock to recover and prevents overgrazing. Additionally, rotational grazing can help to distribute manure more evenly, providing a natural source of fertilizer for your crops.

Promoting Pollination and Biodiversity

Wildlife, particularly pollinators such as bees, butterflies, and hummingbirds, play a vital role in the success of your permaculture system. By providing food, water, and shelter for these species, you can encourage their presence and increase the productivity of your crops.

To promote pollination and biodiversity, consider the following strategies:

- Plant diverse flowering plants, including native species that bloom at different times throughout the year.
- Provide water sources, such as shallow dishes or birdbaths, for pollinators to drink.
- Leave some areas of your land undisturbed, allowing for natural habitats to form and support a variety of wildlife species.

Monitoring and Adapting to Changing Conditions

Managing livestock and wildlife interactions requires ongoing observation and adaptation. Regularly monitor the health of your animals, the condition of your land, and the presence of wildlife to identify any potential issues or conflicts. By staying attuned to the needs of your permaculture system, you can make adjustments as needed to maintain a harmonious and productive environment.

In conclusion, integrating livestock and wildlife into your permaculture system can lead to numerous long-term benefits, including natural pest control, improved soil health, and increased crop productivity. By carefully managing these interactions and creating a supportive environment for both livestock and wildlife, you can cultivate a thriving and sustainable ecosystem.

Addressing Challenges and Conflicts Between Livestock and Wildlife

In an ideal permaculture system, livestock and wildlife coexist harmoniously, each contributing to the overall health and productivity of the ecosystem. However, it is essential to recognize that challenges and conflicts may arise between these two groups. In this section, we will discuss some common issues and provide practical solutions to ensure a balanced and thriving environment for both livestock and wildlife.

One of the most common challenges in integrating livestock and wildlife is predation. Predators such as foxes, coyotes, and birds of prey can threaten your livestock, particularly smaller animals like chickens and rabbits. To protect your livestock from predators, consider implementing the following strategies:

- Provide secure and well-constructed animal housing, ensuring that all potential entry points are covered and reinforced.
- Employ guardian animals, such as dogs, llamas, or donkeys, to deter predators and protect your livestock.
- Install fencing or other barriers to keep predators out of your property. Electric fencing can be particularly effective in deterring larger predators.
- Encourage the presence of natural predators of smaller predators, such as owls and hawks, by providing nesting boxes and perches.

Another challenge in integrating livestock and wildlife is competition for resources like food and water. To minimize competition and ensure that both groups have access to the resources they need, consider the following strategies:

- Plant a diverse range of forage species to provide ample food for both livestock and wildlife. This can include grasses, legumes, and other plants that provide both nutrition and habitat for various species.
- Establish separate feeding and watering stations for livestock and wildlife, ensuring each group has access to clean and uncontaminated resources.
- Rotate your livestock through different areas of your property, allowing forage to regrow and preventing overgrazing.

Disease transmission between livestock and wildlife is another concern that must be addressed when integrating these two groups. To minimize the risk of disease transmission, consider the following strategies:

- Maintain a healthy and diverse ecosystem, which can help prevent disease spread by supporting a robust population of beneficial insects, birds, and other wildlife.
- Implement biosecurity measures, such as quarantining new animals and regularly monitoring the health of your livestock.
- Encourage natural pest control by providing a habitat for beneficial insects and predators, such as ladybugs, lacewings, and birds.

Lastly, it is crucial to address any legal or regulatory challenges that may arise when integrating livestock and wildlife. Be sure to research and comply with any local, state, or federal regulations regarding the management of wildlife and livestock on your property.

In conclusion, addressing challenges and conflicts between livestock and wildlife is crucial to creating a successful permaculture system. By implementing practical solutions and maintaining a proactive approach to management, you can ensure a harmonious and productive environment for both groups, ultimately contributing to the long-term sustainability and resilience of your permaculture system.

The Long-term Benefits of Integrating Livestock and Wildlife in Permaculture

In conclusion, integrating livestock and wildlife in permaculture systems offers many long-term benefits that contribute to our environment's overall health and sustainability. By fostering a symbiotic relationship between these two essential components, we can create a thriving ecosystem that benefits not only the plants and animals within it but also the people who depend on it for their livelihood and well-being.

One of the most significant long-term benefits of integrating livestock and wildlife in permaculture is **biodiversity enhancement**. By providing a variety of habitats and resources for different species, we can support a rich and diverse community of plants, animals, and microorganisms. This biodiversity, in turn, contributes to the resilience of the ecosystem, enabling it to better withstand disturbances and adapt to changing conditions.

Another long-term benefit is the improvement of soil health and fertility. Livestock and wildlife play a crucial role in cycling nutrients and organic matter through the ecosystem, helping to build and maintain healthy, fertile soils. This not only supports the growth of more robust and productive plants but also helps to sequester carbon and mitigate the impacts of climate change.

Integrating livestock and wildlife in permaculture systems also contributes to pest management and disease control. Encouraging diverse species can create a more balanced ecosystem where natural predators help keep pest populations in check. This reduces the need for harmful chemical pesticides and promotes a healthier environment for all.

Moreover, the integration of livestock and wildlife can provide valuable economic benefits for farmers and landowners. They can build a more resilient and sustainable business model by diversifying their operations and incorporating multiple income streams, such as meat, dairy, eggs, and ecotourism. This, in turn, supports local economies and contributes to food security in the community.

Lastly, integrating livestock and wildlife in permaculture systems fosters a deeper connection between humans and the natural world. By working in harmony with nature, we can cultivate a greater appreciation for the intricate web of life that sustains us and develop a more profound sense of stewardship for the land and its inhabitants.

In summary, the long-term benefits of integrating livestock and wildlife in permaculture are vast and far-reaching. By embracing this holistic approach, we can create healthier, more resilient ecosystems that support a diverse array of species, improve soil health, and contribute to the well-being of both humans and the environment. As we continue to face the challenges of a rapidly changing world, the principles of permaculture offer a guiding light towards a more sustainable and harmonious future.

Chapter Summary

- Integrating livestock and wildlife in permaculture systems is essential for creating a sustainable and thriving ecosystem, as it fosters a symbiotic relationship between domesticated animals and their wild counterparts.
- Choosing the right livestock for your permaculture system involves considering your needs and goals, climate, available space, and experience with handling animals.
- Creating habitats for wildlife to thrive is crucial for maintaining a balanced and diverse landscape, which can be achieved by providing food, water, shelter, and connectivity for various species.
- Managing livestock and wildlife interactions for mutual benefit includes encouraging natural pest control, practicing rotational grazing for soil health, promoting pollination and biodiversity, and monitoring and adapting to changing conditions.

- Addressing challenges and conflicts between livestock and wildlife, such as predation, competition for resources, and disease transmission, is vital for maintaining a harmonious and productive environment.
- Complying with legal and regulatory requirements is essential when integrating livestock and wildlife in permaculture systems.
- The long-term benefits of integrating livestock and wildlife in permaculture include enhanced biodiversity, improved soil health and fertility, natural pest management and disease control, economic benefits for farmers and landowners, and fostering a deeper connection between humans and the natural world.
- Embracing the principles of permaculture and integrating livestock and wildlife can help create healthier, more resilient ecosystems that support a diverse array of species and contribute to the well-being of both humans and the environment.

8

NATURAL PEST CONTROL AND MANAGEMENT

Ladybugs and lacewings teaming up to protect a vibrant garden from aphids and other pests.

In the world of permaculture, the concept of working with nature rather than against it is a fundamental principle. As we strive to create sustainable and self-sufficient ecosystems, one of the most significant challenges we face is **managing pests** in a way that aligns with our commitment to environmental stewardship. Enter the realm of natural pest control and management, a holistic approach that seeks to harness the power of nature to keep pests in check and maintain the balance of our gardens and landscapes.

At first glance, natural pest control and management might seem counterintuitive. After all, aren't pests the very thing we're trying to eliminate from our gardens? However, the key is understanding that not all insects and organisms are harmful. In fact, many play crucial roles in maintaining the health and vitality of our ecosystems. By focusing on promoting the presence of these beneficial creatures and employing organic techniques to deter pests, we can create a thriving permaculture garden that is both productive and ecologically sound.

This chapter will explore the fascinating world of natural pest control and management, exploring the principles and practices that can help you transform your garden into a harmonious and balanced ecosystem. We'll begin by examining the importance of understanding the ecosystem and the role of beneficial insects in maintaining equilibrium.

Next, we'll discuss various organic pest control techniques and strategies that can be employed to minimize the impact of harmful pests on your garden. We'll also cover the concept of companion planting, a powerful tool for managing pests through strategic plant selection and placement. Finally, we'll discuss the importance of monitoring and maintaining a healthy permaculture garden, ensuring that your efforts in natural pest control and management continue to yield positive results.

As we embark on this journey, remember that the goal is not to wage war on pests but to embrace nature's wisdom and work in harmony with the intricate web of life that sustains us all. By adopting a natural approach to pest control and management, you'll contribute to your garden's health and the planet's well-being as a whole. So let's get started, and discover the incredible potential of natural pest control and management in the world of practical permaculture.

Understanding the Ecosystem and Beneficial Insects

In order to effectively implement natural pest control and management in your permaculture garden, it is essential to first understand the ecosystem and the role of beneficial insects. By gaining a deeper comprehension of the intricate relationships between plants, insects, and other organisms, you can harness nature's wisdom to create a thriving, balanced garden that minimizes the need for synthetic pesticides and other harmful interventions.

The ecosystem within your garden is a **complex web of interactions** between various living organisms, including plants, insects, birds, and microorganisms. Each of these components plays a vital role in maintaining the overall health and balance of the garden. In particular, beneficial insects are crucial allies in your quest for natural pest control and management.

Beneficial insects can be divided into two main categories: **predators** and **pollinators**. Predatory insects, such as ladybugs, lacewings, and predatory mites, help control pest populations by feeding on common garden pests like aphids, mites, and caterpillars. These natural predators are essential to any healthy ecosystem and can significantly reduce the need for chemical pesticides.

Pollinators, on the other hand, are essential for the reproduction and growth of many plants. Insects like bees, butterflies, and certain beetles play a crucial role in transferring pollen from one flower to another, allowing plants to produce fruits and seeds. You can ensure a bountiful harvest and a vibrant, thriving garden by attracting and supporting a diverse range of pollinators.

To effectively utilize beneficial insects in your permaculture garden, it's important to create a **welcoming environment** that supports their needs. This can be achieved by:

- Planting diverse flowering plants that provide nectar and pollen for pollinators throughout the growing season.
- Providing habitat for beneficial insects, such as shrubs, trees, and ground cover, where they can find shelter, reproduce, and overwinter.
- Avoid synthetic pesticides, which can harm pests and beneficial insects. Instead, opt for organic pest control methods that target specific pests while minimizing harm to beneficial insects.
- Introducing beneficial insects to your garden, either by purchasing them from a reputable supplier or by attracting them through specific plants and habitat features.

By understanding the ecosystem and the role of beneficial insects, you can create a permaculture garden that works in harmony with nature rather than against it. This approach not only leads to a healthier, more productive garden but also contributes to the overall well-being of our planet. The following sections will explore various organic pest control techniques and strategies to help you maintain a balanced and thriving permaculture garden.

Organic Pest Control Techniques and Strategies

In this section, we will delve into the world of organic pest control techniques and strategies that are both effective and environmentally friendly. These methods not only help maintain the balance of your permaculture garden but also contribute to the overall health of the ecosystem. By adopting these techniques, you can manage pests without resorting to harmful chemical pesticides, ensuring a safe and thriving environment for all living beings in your garden.

Biological Control: One of the most effective organic pest control methods is introducing natural predators and parasites into your garden. These beneficial insects, such as ladybugs, lacewings, and parasitic wasps, can help keep pest populations in check by preying on them or laying their eggs inside the pests. To attract these helpful insects, plant a variety of flowering plants that provide nectar and pollen, and consider purchasing and releasing them in your garden if they are not naturally present.

Physical Barriers: Erecting physical barriers can effectively prevent pests from accessing your plants. Examples of such barriers include floating row covers, which can be placed over your plants to protect them from flying insects, and copper tape, which can be wrapped around the base of plants to deter slugs and snails. Additionally, using netting or fencing can help keep larger pests, such as rabbits and deer, at bay.

Cultural Practices: Adopting certain cultural practices can help reduce the likelihood of pest infestations. For instance, practicing crop rotation can disrupt the life cycle of pests that are specific to certain plants, while proper sanitation, like removing dead leaves and debris, can eliminate potential hiding places for pests. Moreover, maintaining healthy soil and providing your plants with the appropriate nutrients can help them better withstand pest attacks.

Mechanical Control: This involves physically removing or trapping pests from your plants. Handpicking pests, such as caterpillars and beetles, can be an effective method for small gardens. For larger infestations, you can use traps, such as yellow sticky traps to catch flying insects or pheromone traps to attract and capture specific pests.

Botanical and Mineral-Based Pesticides: In cases where other organic pest control methods are insufficient, you can opt for botanical and mineral-based pesticides. These are derived from natural sources and are generally less harmful to the environment than synthetic chemical pesticides. Examples include neem oil, which can control a variety of pests, and diatomaceous earth, which can be used to control crawling insects. However, it is essential to use these products judiciously and follow the label instructions to minimize any potential harm to beneficial insects.

By implementing these organic pest control techniques and strategies, you can create a balanced and healthy permaculture garden that can thrive without the need for harmful chemicals. In the next section, we will explore the concept of companion planting and how it can further enhance your garden's pest management efforts.

Implementing Companion Planting for Pest Management

In the world of permaculture, **companion planting** is a time-tested and highly effective strategy for managing pests naturally and sustainably. By harnessing the power of plant relationships and synergies, you can create a thriving garden ecosystem less susceptible to pest infestations and more resilient in the face of challenges. In this section, we will explore the principles of companion planting, discuss some popular plant combinations, and offer practical tips for implementing this strategy in your own permaculture garden.

Companion planting is based on the idea that certain plants can benefit each other when grown in close proximity. This can happen in several ways, such as attracting beneficial insects, repelling pests, or providing support and nutrients to neighboring plants. The key to successful companion planting is understanding the specific needs and characteristics of each plant species and selecting companions that complement and enhance their growth.

One of the most common uses of companion planting in permaculture is to attract beneficial insects that prey on pests. For example, planting flowers like marigolds, calendula, and yarrow near your vegetable crops can draw in ladybugs, lacewings, and parasitic wasps, which are natural predators of aphids, caterpillars, and other common garden pests. By providing a habitat for these helpful insects, you can reduce the need for chemical pesticides and promote a more balanced and diverse ecosystem.

Another critical aspect of companion planting is choosing plants that repel or deter pests. Some plants emit strong odors or contain unappealing or toxic compounds to certain insects, making them effective natural pest control agents. For instance, planting garlic or onions near lettuce can help keep aphids at bay, while basil planted alongside tomatoes can deter tomato hornworms. Similarly, intercropping your garden with strong-smelling herbs like mint, rosemary, and thyme can confuse and repel a wide range of pests, protecting your valuable crops from damage.

In addition to these direct pest control benefits, companion planting can also improve your garden's overall health and productivity by fostering beneficial plant relationships. For example, planting nitrogen-fixing legumes like beans and peas near heavy feeders like corn and squash can help improve soil fertility and reduce the need for synthetic fertilizers. Similarly, planting tall, sturdy plants like sunflowers or corn can provide natural support and shade for vining or low-growing plants like beans and cucumbers, creating a more efficient and harmonious garden layout.

To implement companion planting in your permaculture garden, start by researching the specific needs and characteristics of your chosen plants and identifying potential companion species that can provide mutual benefits. Then, plan your garden layout with these relationships in mind, grouping compatible plants together and considering factors like sunlight, water, and nutrient requirements. Be prepared to experiment and adjust your plantings as you observe the results and learn from your garden's unique ecosystem.

In conclusion, companion planting is a powerful and practical tool for managing pests and promoting a healthy, productive permaculture garden. By understanding and embracing the natural relationships between plants, you can harness nature's wisdom to create a more resilient and sustainable gardening system. So, go ahead and explore the world of companion planting, and watch your garden flourish in harmony with the environment.

Monitoring and Maintaining a Healthy Permaculture Garden

A thriving permaculture garden is a delicate balance of various elements working in harmony with nature. It is crucial to monitor and maintain your garden's health regularly to ensure its success. This section will guide you through the essential steps to keep your permaculture garden flourishing and effectively manage pests using natural methods.

First and foremost, **observation is vital.** Regularly walk through your garden and observe the plants, insects, and overall health of the ecosystem. This will help you identify any potential issues before they escalate, such as signs of pest infestations, diseases, or nutrient deficiencies. Make a habit of inspecting your garden at least once a week or more frequently during critical growth periods or when introducing new plants or techniques.

One essential aspect of maintaining a healthy permaculture garden is ensuring proper soil health. Healthy soil is the foundation of a thriving ecosystem, as it provides the necessary nutrients and support for plants to grow. Regularly test your soil to monitor its pH levels, nutrient content, and structure. Amend the soil with organic matter, such as compost or well-rotted manure, to maintain its fertility and structure. Additionally, practice crop rotation and cover cropping to prevent nutrient depletion and soil-borne diseases.

Another crucial factor in maintaining a healthy garden is proper watering. Overwatering or underwatering can lead to stressed plants, making them more susceptible to pests and diseases. Observe the moisture levels in your soil and adjust your watering schedule accordingly. Utilize drip irrigation or rainwater harvesting techniques to conserve water and ensure that your plants receive the appropriate amount of moisture.

Pruning and trimming plants is also an essential part of garden maintenance. Regularly remove dead or diseased plant material to prevent the spread of diseases and pests. Pruning also promotes air circulation and sunlight penetration, which are vital for plant health and growth. Be sure to sanitize your pruning tools between uses to avoid spreading diseases.

Attracting and supporting beneficial insects is a cornerstone of natural pest control in a permaculture garden. Encourage these helpful creatures by providing diverse plants, including flowering species that produce nectar and pollen. Additionally, consider installing insect hotels or nesting boxes to provide shelter and breeding sites for beneficial insects.

Finally, be prepared to intervene when necessary. Despite your best efforts, some pests may still find their way into your garden. In such cases, act promptly and use organic pest control methods, such as introducing predatory insects, using insecticidal soaps, or applying natural repellents like neem oil. Always opt for the least harmful method first, and do not escalate unless it is required.

In conclusion, monitoring and maintaining a healthy permaculture garden is an ongoing process that requires patience, observation, and a deep understanding of the natural ecosystem. By embracing nature's wisdom and working in harmony with it, you can create a thriving garden that effectively manages pests and contributes to a sustainable future.

Embracing Nature's Wisdom in Pest Control and Management

As we reach the end of this enlightening journey through natural pest control and management, it is essential to reflect on the wisdom that nature has to offer. Throughout this chapter, we have explored the importance of understanding the ecosystem, the role of beneficial insects, organic pest control techniques, and the power of companion planting. All these elements work together to create a harmonious and healthy permaculture garden that thrives without the need for harmful chemicals.

Embracing nature's wisdom in pest control and management means recognizing that our gardens are not isolated entities but are part of a larger ecosystem. By working with nature rather than against it, we can create an environment where pests are kept in check by natural predators and plants that support each other's growth. This approach not only benefits our plants but also contributes to the overall health of our environment and the planet.

One of the most important aspects of natural pest control and management is the **willingness to learn from nature**. Observing the interactions between plants, insects, and other organisms in our gardens can provide valuable insights into how we can best support the health and productivity of our plants. By adopting a holistic approach to pest management, we can minimize the need for intervention and create a self-sustaining garden that thrives with minimal input from us.

In conclusion, the principles of practical permaculture encourage us to work with nature to create a sustainable and productive garden. By understanding the ecosystem, harnessing the power of beneficial insects, implementing organic pest control techniques, and utilizing companion planting, we can create a garden that is not only beautiful but also resilient and self-sustaining. Embracing nature's wisdom in pest control and management is a practical approach to gardening and a testament to our commitment to preserving the environment for future generations.

As you continue your journey in permaculture, remember to always be open to learning from nature, observing the intricate relationships between organisms, and seeking innovative ways to create a harmonious and thriving garden. With patience, dedication, and deep respect for the natural world, you will undoubtedly reap the rewards of a flourishing permaculture garden that is both productive and sustainable.

Chapter Summary

- Natural pest control and management is a holistic approach that works with nature to maintain a balanced and healthy garden ecosystem, minimizing the need for synthetic pesticides and other harmful interventions.
- Understanding the ecosystem and the role of beneficial insects, such as predators and pollinators, is crucial for effective natural pest control and management in a permaculture garden.
- Organic pest control techniques and strategies, including biological control, physical barriers, cultural practices, mechanical control, and botanical and mineral-based pesticides, can help manage pests without resorting to harmful chemicals.
- Companion planting is a powerful tool for managing pests through strategic plant selection and placement, harnessing the power of plant relationships and synergies to create a thriving garden ecosystem.
- Regular monitoring and maintaining a healthy permaculture garden is essential for its success, involving observation, proper soil health, appropriate watering, pruning, and supporting beneficial insects.

- Attracting and supporting beneficial insects is a cornerstone of natural pest control in a permaculture garden, achieved by providing a diverse range of plants and installing insect hotels or nesting boxes.
- Embracing nature's wisdom in pest control and management means recognizing that gardens are part of a larger ecosystem and working with nature to create an environment where pests are kept in check by natural predators and supportive plants.
- By adopting a holistic approach to pest management and learning from nature, we can create a self-sustaining garden that thrives with minimal input, contributing to the overall health of our environment and the planet.

9

PERMACULTURE IN URBAN AND SMALL SPACES

An enchanting urban rooftop garden, incorporating elements of permaculture such as vertical planting, rainwater harvesting, and companion planting, to create a lush green oasis amidst the concrete jungle.

Permaculture is a holistic approach to sustainable living that integrates ecological design, resource conservation, and self-reliance. While it may be easy to envision permaculture principles being applied to sprawling rural landscapes, embracing these concepts in urban and small spaces is equally essential and possible. In this chapter, we will explore the myriad ways in which permaculture can be adapted to fit the unique challenges and opportunities presented by limited spaces.

The world is becoming increasingly urbanized, with more than half the global population residing in cities. This trend is expected to continue, making it essential for *urban dwellers* to find innovative ways to grow food, conserve resources, and build resilient communities in the face of climate change and other challenges. Permaculture offers a powerful framework for achieving these goals, even in the most cramped and concrete-laden environments.

Adopting a mindset of creativity, flexibility, and resourcefulness in embracing permaculture in limited spaces is crucial. This means looking beyond traditional gardening methods and embracing innovative techniques such as vertical gardening, multi-functional elements, and urban food forests. It also involves recognizing the value of community connections and the potential for integrating small-scale livestock into urban ecosystems.

This chapter will delve into these topics and provide practical guidance for implementing permaculture principles in urban and small spaces. By doing so, we aim to empower readers to transform their balconies, rooftops, and tiny backyards into thriving, resilient ecosystems that contribute to the health and well-being of both people and the planet.

In the following sections, we will explore the diverse ways in which permaculture can be adapted to urban and small spaces, from maximizing space through vertical gardening and multi-functional elements to creating edible landscapes and fostering community connections. We will also discuss the potential for integrating small-scale livestock into urban permaculture systems, highlighting the benefits and challenges of doing so. By the end of this chapter, readers will be equipped with the knowledge and inspiration needed to embrace permaculture in their own limited spaces, transforming them into thriving, sustainable ecosystems.

Maximizing Space: Vertical Gardening and Multi-Functional Elements

In the world of permaculture, creativity knows no bounds, especially when it comes to maximizing space in urban and small-scale settings. With limited room to work with, it's essential to think outside the box and utilize every inch of available space. In this section, we'll explore two critical strategies for making the most of your urban or small-space permaculture garden: **vertical gardening** and **multi-functional elements.**

Vertical Gardening

When horizontal space is scarce, it's time to look up and embrace the concept of **vertical gardening.** This innovative approach allows you to grow plants on walls, trellises, and other vertical structures, effectively multiplying your garden's square footage without expanding its footprint. Vertical gardening saves space and offers numerous benefits, such as improved air circulation, easier pest control, and increased exposure to sunlight for your plants.

To get started with vertical gardening, consider the following techniques:

Trellises and Climbing Plants: Install trellises or other support structures for climbing plants like beans, peas, cucumbers, and even some varieties of tomatoes. These plants will naturally grow upwards, making the most of your vertical space.

Wall Planters: Attach planters to walls, fences, or other vertical surfaces to create a living wall of herbs, flowers, or even small fruiting plants like strawberries. This not only maximizes space but also adds visual interest to your garden.

Pallet Gardens: Repurpose wooden pallets by filling them with soil and planting a variety of shallow-rooted plants in the gaps between the slats. Stand the pallets upright against a wall or fence for an instant vertical garden.

Hanging Baskets: Suspend hanging baskets from balconies, eaves, or other overhead structures to grow trailing plants like nasturtiums, cherry tomatoes, or even small fruit trees.

Multi-Functional Elements

Another key strategy for maximizing space in your urban or small-space permaculture garden is to incorporate **multi-functional elements.** These are features that serve more than one purpose, effectively increasing the efficiency and productivity of your garden without taking up additional space.

Here are some examples of multi-functional elements you can incorporate into your garden:

1. **Edible Landscaping:** Replace purely ornamental plants with edible varieties that provide both beauty and sustenance. For example, plant fruit trees or berry bushes instead of non-fruiting ornamentals or use edible ground covers like creeping thyme or oregano instead of traditional lawn grasses.

2. **Living Fences:** Instead of installing a standard wooden or metal fence, consider planting a hedge of fruiting shrubs or trees, like raspberries or hazelnuts. This not only provides a natural barrier but also offers food and habitat for wildlife.

3. **Rainwater Harvesting:** Collect rainwater from your roof or other surfaces using gutters, downspouts, and rain barrels. This water can then be used to irrigate your garden, reducing your reliance on municipal water supplies and lowering your water bill.

4. **Composting Systems:** Turn kitchen scraps and yard waste into valuable fertilizer by setting up a composting system in your garden. This not only reduces the amount of waste sent to landfills but also provides a steady supply of nutrient-rich compost for your plants.

You can make the most of every available space by embracing vertical gardening and incorporating multi-functional elements into your urban or small-space permaculture garden. In doing so, you'll create a thriving, productive oasis that not only nourishes your body and soul but also contributes to the health and resilience of your local ecosystem.

Urban Food Forests: Creating Edible Landscapes in the City

As cities continue to grow and expand, the need for sustainable and efficient food production becomes increasingly important. Urban food forests offer a unique and innovative solution to this challenge, transforming underutilized spaces into thriving, edible landscapes. In this section, we will explore the concept of urban food forests, their benefits, and how you can create your own edible oasis in the heart of the city.

At its core, an urban food forest is a carefully designed ecosystem that **mimics the structure and function of a natural forest** while providing a diverse array of edible plants. By integrating fruit and nut trees, berry bushes, perennial vegetables, and herbs, these landscapes not only produce food but also provide habitat for wildlife, improve air and water quality, and create a sense of community among city dwellers.

One of the most significant benefits of urban food forests is their ability to produce a high yield of diverse crops in a relatively small area. By utilizing vertical space through the planting of trees, shrubs, and groundcovers, these gardens can produce an abundance of food without the need for large tracts of land. This makes them an ideal solution for urban environments where space is often limited.

Creating an urban food forest begins with careful planning and design. Start by assessing the available space, sunlight, and soil conditions to determine which plants will thrive in your location. Next, consider the various layers of a forest ecosystem – the canopy, understory, shrub layer, herbaceous layer, and ground cover – and select plants that will fill each of these roles. Doing so will create a diverse and resilient system that can withstand pests, diseases, and changing environmental conditions.

When selecting plants for your urban food forest, prioritize native species and those that are well-adapted to your local climate. This will ensure that your garden is low-maintenance and supports local biodiversity. Additionally, choose plants that offer multiple functions, such as nitrogen-fixing legumes that improve soil fertility or fruit trees that provide shade and habitat for birds.

Once your urban food forest is established, it will require minimal intervention to maintain its productivity. Regular pruning, mulching, and occasional watering may be necessary, but the self-sustaining nature of these ecosystems means that they will largely take care of themselves. As the food forest matures, it will become a lush, abundant space that provides food, beauty, and tranquility in the heart of the city.

In conclusion, urban food forests represent a powerful and transformative approach to urban agriculture and permaculture. By harnessing the principles of natural ecosystems and applying them to our city landscapes, we can create abundant, resilient, and beautiful spaces that nourish both people and the planet. So, whether you have a small backyard or a vacant lot, consider the potential of an urban food forest to transform your space into a thriving, edible landscape.

Community Connections: Building Resilience through Local Networks

In the realm of urban and small-space permaculture, the power of community connections cannot be overstated. As we strive to create sustainable, resilient, and vibrant ecosystems in our limited spaces, we must recognize that we are not isolated entities. Instead, we are part of a larger network of individuals, families, and organizations, all of whom can contribute to the success of our permaculture endeavors. In this section, we will explore the importance of building and nurturing local networks to enhance the resilience of our urban and small-space permaculture projects.

The concept of community connections in permaculture is rooted in the understanding that **we are stronger when we work together**. By pooling our resources, knowledge, and skills, we can create more robust and adaptable systems that are better equipped to withstand the challenges of urban living and the uncertainties of our changing world. In practical terms, this means engaging with our neighbors, local organizations, and fellow permaculture enthusiasts to share ideas, collaborate on projects, and support one another in our journey toward a more sustainable future.

One of the most effective ways to build community connections in urban and small-space permaculture is by **establishing local gardening and permaculture groups.** These groups can serve as a platform for individuals to come together to learn from one another, share resources, and collaborate on projects that benefit the entire community. Participating in such groups gives you access to a wealth of knowledge and experience to help you overcome the unique challenges of practicing permaculture in limited spaces.

Another powerful tool for fostering community connections is the **organization of local events**, such as workshops, skill-sharing sessions, and garden tours. These events not only provide valuable learning opportunities but also help to strengthen the bonds between community members and create a sense of shared purpose. Additionally, they can serve as a means of raising awareness about permaculture and its potential benefits for urban and small-space dwellers.

In addition to these formalized groups and events, it is essential to cultivate informal connections with our neighbors and fellow community members. Simple acts such as sharing surplus produce, offering assistance with garden tasks, or exchanging seeds and plant cuttings can go a long way in building trust and fostering a sense of camaraderie.

These informal connections can also lead to more significant collaborations, such as establishing community gardens, creating shared composting systems, or developing neighborhood-wide initiatives to promote sustainable living.

In conclusion, community connections are vital to urban and small-space permaculture. By building and nurturing local networks, we can tap into our community's collective wisdom, resources, and skills, making our permaculture projects more resilient and successful. Furthermore, these connections help to create a sense of belonging and shared purpose, fostering a culture of sustainability and cooperation that extends far beyond the boundaries of our individual gardens and homes.

Small-Scale Livestock: Integrating Animals into Urban Permaculture

When we think of permaculture, we often envision sprawling gardens and vast landscapes teeming with plant life. However, a crucial component of permaculture often overlooked is the integration of small-scale livestock. This section will explore the benefits of incorporating animals into urban permaculture systems and discuss how to do so effectively and ethically.

First, let's address why animals are included in urban permaculture. The answer lies in the symbiotic relationship between plants and animals. Animals can provide valuable services to your garden, such as pest control, fertilization, and soil aeration. In return, your garden offers these creatures food, shelter, and natural habitat. This mutually beneficial relationship not only enhances the productivity of your garden but also promotes biodiversity and ecological balance.

Now, let's dive into some practical ways to integrate small-scale livestock into your urban permaculture system:

Chickens: These feathered friends are a popular choice for urban permaculture enthusiasts. Chickens can help control pests by eating insects, weeds, and kitchen scraps. They also produce nutrient-rich manure that can be used as fertilizer. Additionally, they provide fresh eggs, a valuable source of protein for your family. When selecting a breed, consider smaller, quieter varieties that are well-suited for urban environments, such as the Bantam or Silkie.

Bees: Urban beekeeping is gaining popularity as more people recognize the importance of pollinators in our ecosystems. Bees not only produce honey but also play a vital role in pollinating plants, ensuring a bountiful harvest. Installing a beehive in your garden can significantly improve the health and productivity of your plants while providing a home for these essential insects.

Rabbits: These small mammals are another excellent addition to your urban permaculture system. Rabbits are efficient at converting plant material into protein and produce high-quality manure that can be used as fertilizer. They can be housed in small hutches and require minimal space, making them ideal for urban settings. Plus, their gentle nature and quiet demeanor make them excellent companions for children and adults alike.

Worms: Vermicomposting, or worm composting, is a fantastic way to recycle kitchen scraps and produce nutrient-rich compost for your garden. Worms break down organic matter, turning it into a valuable soil amendment called "worm castings." This process not only reduces waste but also improves soil structure and fertility. A simple worm bin can be set up in a small space, such as a balcony or garage, making it an ideal option for urban permaculture practitioners.

Fish: Aquaponics is an innovative method of growing plants and fish together in a closed-loop system. The fish waste provides nutrients for the plants, while the plants filter the water, creating a clean environment for the fish. This symbiotic relationship allows for the efficient use of space and resources, making it an attractive option for urban permaculture enthusiasts.

In conclusion, integrating small-scale livestock into your urban permaculture system can provide numerous benefits, from increased garden productivity to enhanced biodiversity. By carefully selecting the right animals for your space and needs, you can create a thriving, sustainable ecosystem that supports both plants and animals. Embrace the transformative power of urban and small-space permaculture by incorporating these living elements into your garden, and watch as your green oasis flourishes.

The Transformative Power of Urban and Small-Space Permaculture

As we reach the end of this enlightening journey through the world of urban and small-space permaculture, it is essential to reflect on the transformative power this practice holds for individuals, communities, and our planet. In a time when urbanization is rapidly expanding and the need for sustainable living practices is more urgent than ever, permaculture offers a beacon of hope and a practical solution to many of the challenges we face.

Throughout this chapter, we have explored various techniques and strategies that enable city dwellers and those with limited space to

embrace permaculture principles. From vertical gardening and multi-functional elements to urban food forests and community connections, these approaches empower individuals to make the most of their available space while contributing to a more sustainable and resilient future.

Integrating small-scale livestock into urban permaculture systems further demonstrates the adaptability and versatility of this practice. By incorporating animals into our urban ecosystems, we not only benefit from their valuable contributions to soil fertility and pest control, but we also foster a deeper connection to the natural world and the cycles of life that sustains us.

Perhaps the most significant aspect of urban and small-space permaculture is its ability to unite people. As we cultivate local networks and collaborate with our neighbors, we create a sense of community and belonging that is often lacking in modern urban environments. This social aspect of permaculture not only strengthens our resilience in the face of adversity but also contributes to our overall well-being and happiness.

In conclusion, the transformative power of urban and small-space permaculture lies in its capacity to inspire change on both a personal and collective level. By embracing these principles and practices, we can create thriving, sustainable ecosystems that nourish our bodies, minds, and souls, while also contributing to the health and vitality of our planet. As more and more people adopt permaculture practices in their urban and small spaces, we move closer to a world where harmony with nature and sustainable living become the norm rather than the exception. So, let us continue to learn, grow, and share our knowledge with others as we work together to create a brighter, greener future for all.

Chapter Summary

- Urban and small-space permaculture is a powerful approach to sustainable living that can be adapted to fit the unique challenges and opportunities presented by limited spaces.

- Vertical gardening and multi-functional elements are key strategies for maximizing space in urban and small-scale settings, allowing for increased productivity and efficiency in limited areas.
- Urban food forests offer a unique and innovative solution to sustainable food production in cities, transforming underutilized spaces into thriving, edible landscapes.
- Building community connections and fostering local networks are essential components of urban and small-space permaculture, contributing to the resilience and success of permaculture projects.
- Small-scale livestock, such as chickens, bees, rabbits, worms, and fish, can be integrated into urban permaculture systems to provide valuable services, promote biodiversity, and enhance garden productivity.
- Permaculture practices in urban and small spaces can bring people together, creating a sense of community and belonging that is often lacking in modern urban environments.
- The transformative power of urban and small-space permaculture lies in its capacity to inspire personal and collective change, contributing to a more sustainable and resilient future.
- As more people adopt permaculture practices in their urban and small spaces, we move closer to a world where harmony with nature and sustainable living become the norm rather than the exception.

10

HARVESTING, PRESERVING, AND SHARING THE ABUNDANCE

A magical vegetable waterfall, with a cascade of various vegetables flowing down a mountainside into a lush, green valley, symbolizing the endless abundance of nature's bounty.

Permaculture is a holistic approach to agriculture and sustainable living that seeks to create a harmonious relationship between humans, plants, animals, and the environment. By designing systems that mimic natural ecosystems, permaculture practitioners aim to produce abundant food, fiber, and energy while minimizing waste and nurturing the health of the land. This chapter will delve into the rewarding process of harvesting, preserving, and sharing the fruits of your permaculture labor.

As you immerse yourself in the world of permaculture, you will quickly discover that the bountiful harvests it yields are not only a **source of nourishment** but also **a symbol of the interconnectedness of all living things.** The abundance that springs forth from a well-designed permaculture system is a testament to the power of working with nature rather than against it. By embracing the principles of permaculture, you are not only cultivating a thriving garden but also fostering a deeper connection to the earth and your community.

The process of harvesting, preserving, and sharing the abundance of your permaculture garden is a celebration of the cycles of life and the generosity of nature. As you learn to recognize the optimal time to harvest each plant, you will develop a keen awareness of the rhythms of the natural world. Preserving the fruits of your labor allows you to extend the life of your harvest, ensuring that you can enjoy the flavors and nutrients of your garden throughout the year. Sharing your bounty with friends, family, and neighbors is an opportunity to strengthen social bonds and spread the message of permaculture to a wider audience.

In this chapter, we will explore the art of harvesting, delving into the best practices for timing and techniques to ensure the highest quality and yield. We will then discuss various methods for preserving your harvest, from traditional techniques like canning and drying to innovative approaches such as fermentation and freezing. Finally, we will examine the importance of sharing the wealth of your permaculture garden, highlighting the ways in which this practice can foster community connections and promote a more sustainable future.

As you embark on this journey of harvesting, preserving, and sharing the abundance of your permaculture garden, remember that you are nurturing your well-being and contributing to the planet's health and vitality. Furthermore, by embracing permaculture principles, you are planting the seeds of a more sustainable, just, and abundant future for all.

The Art of Harvesting: Timing and Techniques

In the world of permaculture, the art of harvesting is a crucial skill that every practitioner must master. Knowing when and how to harvest your crops ensures that you reap the maximum benefits from your garden while maintaining the health and vitality of your plants. In this section, we will explore the importance of proper timing and techniques in harvesting, allowing you to fully embrace the abundance of permaculture.

Timing is Everything

One of the most critical aspects of harvesting is knowing when to do it. The ideal time to harvest varies depending on the crop type, the weather, and the specific needs of your garden. Here are some general guidelines to help you determine the best time to harvest your produce:

Observe your plants: Pay close attention to the appearance of your crops. Look for signs of ripeness, such as a change in color, size, or texture. For example, tomatoes are ready to harvest when they have a deep red color and a slightly soft texture.

Taste test: Sampling a small portion of your produce can help you determine if it's ready to harvest. The taste should be flavorful and not bitter or bland.

Monitor the weather: Weather conditions can significantly impact the quality of your harvest. Generally, it's best to harvest in the early morning or late afternoon when temperatures are more relaxed. This helps to preserve the freshness and flavor of your produce.

Consider the plant's lifecycle: Some plants, such as leafy greens, can be harvested multiple times throughout their lifecycle. In these cases, it's essential to harvest in a way that promotes continued growth and production.

Mastering the Techniques

Once you've determined the optimal time to harvest your crops, it's essential to use the proper techniques to ensure the health of your plants and the quality of your produce. Here are some essential harvesting techniques to keep in mind:

Use clean, sharp tools: Dull or dirty tools can damage your plants and introduce harmful pathogens. Therefore, ensure that your harvesting tools, such as knives, scissors, or pruners, are clean and sharp before use.

Be gentle: When harvesting, handle your produce with care to avoid bruising or damaging the fruits and vegetables. This not only preserves the quality of your harvest but also helps to prevent the spread of disease.

Harvest selectively: Instead of harvesting an entire plant at once, consider selectively picking the ripest fruits or leaves. This allows the plant to continue producing and encourages a more extended harvest season.

Leave some behind: In the spirit of permaculture, consider leaving a small portion of your harvest behind for wildlife, insects, and natural decomposition. This helps to support the ecosystem and contributes to the overall health of your garden.

By mastering the art of harvesting, you can ensure that you are making the most of the abundance that your permaculture garden has to offer. By paying close attention to timing and using proper techniques, you can enjoy a bountiful and sustainable harvest that nourishes both your body and the environment.

Preserving Your Harvest: Methods for Longevity and Quality

As the fruits of your permaculture labor begin to ripen and fill your garden with an array of colors, flavors, and textures, it's time to consider the best ways to preserve your harvest. By employing various preservation techniques, you can extend the life of your produce, reduce food waste, and enjoy the fruits of your labor throughout the year. This section will explore several methods for preserving your harvest, ensuring both longevity and quality.

Drying: Drying is one of the oldest and most straightforward methods of preserving food. By removing the moisture from your produce, you inhibit the growth of bacteria and mold, thus prolonging its shelf life. There are several ways to dry your harvest, including air drying, oven drying, and using a food dehydrator. Herbs, fruits, and vegetables can all be dried and stored in airtight containers for future use. Additionally, dried foods are lightweight and easy to transport, making them perfect for camping trips or as emergency provisions.

Canning: Canning is another popular method for preserving your harvest. By sealing your produce in airtight containers and subjecting them to high temperatures, you can effectively kill any bacteria or microorganisms that may cause spoilage. There are two primary methods of canning: water bath canning and pressure canning. Water bath canning is suitable for high-acid foods such as fruits, pickles, and jams, while pressure canning is necessary for low-acid foods like vegetables and meats. Canned goods can last for years when stored in a cool, dark place, providing you with a reliable source of nutritious food.

Freezing: Freezing is a quick and easy way to preserve your harvest, particularly for fruits and vegetables that may not be suitable for drying or canning. By freezing your produce at its peak ripeness, you can lock in its flavor and nutritional content. It's essential to blanch vegetables before freezing to preserve their color, texture, and nutritional value. Fruits can be frozen whole or sliced, with or without added sugar. Remember to use proper freezer-safe containers to prevent freezer burn and ensure the quality of your preserved produce.

Fermenting: Fermentation is a natural process that transforms your harvest into a flavorful, probiotic-rich food. By creating an anaerobic environment, beneficial bacteria can thrive and preserve your produce by converting sugars into lactic acid. Some popular fermented foods include sauerkraut, kimchi, pickles, and yogurt. Fermenting your harvest not only extends its shelf life but also enhances its nutritional content and adds a unique depth of flavor.

Root Cellaring: Root cellaring is a traditional method of storing fruits and vegetables in a cool, dark, and humid environment. This method relies on the earth's natural properties to maintain a stable temperature and humidity level, slowing the ripening process and preserving your harvest for an extended period. Root cellaring is ideal for storing root vegetables, winter squash, apples, and pears. By creating a dedicated space for root cellaring, you can keep your harvest fresh and accessible throughout the winter months.

In conclusion, preserving your harvest is an essential aspect of permaculture, allowing you to enjoy the fruits of your labor year-round and reduce food waste. By employing various preservation techniques, you can ensure the longevity and quality of your produce while adding diversity to your diet. As you continue to explore the world of permaculture, remember that preserving your harvest is just as important as growing it, and together, they contribute to a sustainable and abundant future.

Sharing the Wealth: Building Community through Permaculture

One of the most rewarding aspects of permaculture is the opportunity to share the fruits of your labor with others. By cultivating an environment that fosters collaboration, generosity, and a sense of belonging, you can create a strong, resilient community that thrives on the principles of permaculture. In this section, we will explore the various ways in which you can share the wealth of your permaculture garden and build a vibrant, interconnected community.

Community Gardens and Allotments: A great way to share the abundance of your permaculture garden is by participating in or establishing a community garden or allotment. These shared spaces provide an opportunity for individuals to come together, learn from one another, and collectively work towards a common goal. They also serve as a platform for sharing resources, knowledge, and skills, fostering a sense of camaraderie and mutual support among participants.

Seed and Plant Swaps: Organizing or attending seed and plant swaps is another excellent way to share the wealth of your permaculture garden.

These events allow gardeners to exchange seeds, seedlings, and plants, promoting biodiversity and encouraging the cultivation of heirlooms and locally adapted varieties. Seed and plant swaps also provide a forum for sharing knowledge and experiences, helping to strengthen the bonds between community members.

Workshops and Skill Shares: Sharing your knowledge and skills is an invaluable way to contribute to your community and promote the principles of permaculture. By offering workshops, demonstrations, or informal skill shares, you can empower others to take control of their own food production and contribute to developing a more sustainable, self-reliant community. Workshop topics might include composting, natural pest control, water harvesting, or food preservation techniques.

Food Donations and Gleaning Programs: Donating surplus produce to local food banks, shelters, or community kitchens is a wonderful way to share the wealth of your permaculture garden with those in need. Gleaning programs, which involve collecting unharvested produce from farms and gardens to distribute to those experiencing food insecurity, are another effective means of sharing the abundance. Participating in these initiatives can help alleviate hunger and promote food justice within your community.

Community Supported Agriculture (CSA) and Food Co-ops: Joining or establishing a Community Supported Agriculture (CSA) program or food co-op is yet another way to share the wealth of your permaculture garden. These models promote a direct relationship between producers and consumers, fostering a sense of shared responsibility and mutual support. Participating in a CSA or food co-op can help create a more equitable, sustainable, and resilient local food system.

In conclusion, sharing the wealth of your permaculture garden is not only a fulfilling and rewarding endeavor but also an essential component of building a strong, interconnected community. By embracing the principles of collaboration, generosity, and mutual support, you can contribute to cultivating a sustainable future that benefits us all.

Cultivating a Sustainable Future through Permaculture

As we reach the end of our journey through harvesting, preserving, and sharing the abundance of permaculture, it is essential to reflect on the broader implications of these practices for our world. The principles of permaculture not only promote a sustainable and self-sufficient lifestyle but also foster a deep connection with nature, our communities, and ourselves. By embracing the tenets of permaculture, we can cultivate a brighter, more resilient future for generations to come.

Throughout this chapter, we have explored the importance of timing and techniques in harvesting, various methods for preserving the fruits of our labor, and the power of sharing our bounty with others. These practices not only provide us with nourishment and sustenance but also serve as a reminder of our interdependence with the earth and its ecosystems. By working in harmony with nature, we can harness its abundance while minimizing our impact on the environment.

Moreover, sharing our harvest with others fosters a sense of community and connection often lacking in today's fast-paced, consumer-driven society. By engaging in collaborative efforts, such as community gardens or food-sharing initiatives, we can strengthen our bonds with neighbors and friends while promoting a more equitable distribution of resources. This spirit of generosity and reciprocity is at the heart of permaculture and serves as a powerful antidote to the isolation and disconnection that many people experience in the modern world.

In conclusion, the principles and practices of permaculture offer a roadmap for cultivating a sustainable future rooted in abundance, resilience, and community. By embracing these values and integrating them into our daily lives, we can create a world where humans and nature can thrive. As we harvest, preserve, and share the fruits of our labor, we are not only nourishing our bodies but also nourishing our souls and the collective spirit of our communities. Together, we can sow the seeds of change and reap the rewards of a more just, equitable, and sustainable world.

Chapter Summary

- Permaculture is a holistic approach to agriculture and sustainable living that focuses on creating a harmonious relationship between humans, plants, animals, and the environment, resulting in abundant food, fiber, and energy production.
- Proper harvesting techniques and timing are crucial for ensuring the highest quality and yield of produce, as well as maintaining the health and vitality of plants.
- Preserving the harvest through various methods, such as drying, canning, freezing, fermenting, and root cellaring, allows for the enjoyment of garden produce throughout the year and reduces food waste.
- Sharing the abundance of a permaculture garden with friends, family, and neighbors strengthens social bonds and promotes the principles of permaculture to a wider audience.
- Community gardens, seed and plant swaps, workshops, food donations, and gleaning programs are all ways to share the wealth of a permaculture garden and build a strong, interconnected community.
- The principles of permaculture not only promote a sustainable and self-sufficient lifestyle but also foster a deep connection with nature, our communities, and ourselves, contributing to a brighter, more resilient future for generations to come.
- By embracing the tenets of permaculture and integrating them into our daily lives, we can create a world where both humans and nature can thrive, fostering a sense of community, generosity, and reciprocity.

THE FUTURE OF PERMACULTURE

As we conclude our permaculture journey, it is essential to take a moment to reflect on the knowledge and insights we have gained throughout this exploration. As we have discovered, permaculture is not merely a set of gardening techniques or a trendy buzzword. It is a holistic approach to living in harmony with nature, creating sustainable systems that benefit both people and the planet. By embracing permaculture principles, we can transform our lives and our environment for the better.

Throughout this book, we have delved into the core concepts of permaculture, examining its ethical foundation and the practical applications of its principles. We have explored the importance of observing and understanding natural patterns and the value of designing systems that mimic these patterns to create resilient and productive ecosystems. From soil health and water management to plant diversity and animal integration, we have learned how permaculture practices can be applied to various aspects of our lives, whether we live on a small urban plot or a sprawling rural farm.

As we have seen, permaculture is not a one-size-fits-all solution but a **flexible framework** that can be adapted to suit individual needs and local conditions. By adopting a permaculture mindset, we can become more mindful of our actions and their consequences, and make informed decisions that promote sustainability and regeneration. This journey has shown us that permaculture is not just about growing food but about cultivating a deeper connection with the natural world and fostering a sense of responsibility for its well-being.

In the following sections, we will explore the broader implications of permaculture for our society and planet. We will discuss how permaculture is shaping the future of agriculture, offering innovative solutions to global environmental challenges, and inspiring a new generation of eco-conscious citizens. We will also examine the role of technology and innovation in advancing permaculture practices and consider how education and community involvement can help to spread the permaculture ethos.

As we conclude our permaculture journey, let us remember that this is not the end but the beginning of a lifelong adventure. By embracing the principles of permaculture, we can continue to learn, grow, and evolve, both as individuals and as a collective, working together to create a more sustainable and harmonious future for all.

The Growing Impact of Permaculture on Modern Agriculture

As we have journeyed through the world of practical permaculture, it has become increasingly evident that this holistic approach to agriculture is not only beneficial for our gardens and homes but also holds the potential to revolutionize modern agriculture. The growing impact of permaculture on today's farming practices is a testament to its effectiveness and sustainability as more and more farmers and agriculturalists embrace its principles.

One of the most significant ways permaculture influences modern agriculture is by promoting **biodiversity** and **ecological balance**. Traditional farming methods often rely on monoculture, which involves the cultivation of a single crop in a given area. While this approach may yield high production levels in the short term, it can lead to soil depletion, increased vulnerability to pests, and a decline in overall ecosystem health. In contrast, permaculture encourages the cultivation of diverse plant species, which not only fosters a more resilient and productive system but also supports the health of the surrounding environment.

Another notable impact of permaculture on modern agriculture is its focus on **regenerative practices**. Conventional farming methods often deplete the soil and contribute to environmental degradation through synthetic fertilizers, pesticides, and intensive tillage. Permaculture, on the other hand, emphasizes the importance of nurturing the soil and preserving its natural fertility. By employing techniques such as composting, mulching, and cover cropping, permaculture practitioners work to replenish the soil's nutrients and promote its long-term health. This shift towards regenerative agriculture not only enhances the land's productivity but also helps mitigate the adverse effects of climate change by sequestering carbon in the soil.

Furthermore, permaculture's emphasis on local, small-scale production is gradually transforming the way we think about agriculture and food systems. In an era of industrial agriculture and globalized food chains, the importance of local, sustainable food production cannot be overstated. Permaculture encourages the development of community-supported agriculture (CSA) initiatives, farmers' markets, and urban gardens, which not only reduce the environmental footprint of our food systems but also foster stronger connections between producers and consumers.

Finally, the growing impact of permaculture on modern agriculture can be seen in the increasing number of educational programs and resources dedicated to its principles. From workshops and online courses to books and documentaries, a wealth of information is available for those interested in learning more about permaculture and its applications. This widespread dissemination of knowledge is crucial for the continued growth and development of permaculture as a viable alternative to conventional agriculture.

In conclusion, the growing impact of permaculture on modern agriculture is a testament to its effectiveness, sustainability, and potential to address some of the most pressing challenges facing our global food systems. By embracing permaculture principles, we can work towards a more resilient, ecologically balanced, and sustainable future for agriculture and our planet.

Permaculture as a Solution to Global Environmental Challenges

As we stand at the precipice of unprecedented environmental challenges, it becomes increasingly evident that our current agricultural practices and consumption patterns are unsustainable. Climate change, deforestation, soil degradation, and water scarcity are just a few of the pressing issues that threaten the future of our planet. In this context, permaculture emerges as a beacon of hope, offering a holistic and regenerative approach to agriculture that can help mitigate these challenges and pave the way for a more sustainable future.

One of the core tenets of permaculture is its emphasis on **working with**, rather than against, **nature**. By mimicking natural ecosystems and promoting biodiversity, permaculture practices can help restore degraded lands and foster resilience in the face of climate change. For instance, agroforestry techniques, which involve integrating trees and shrubs into agricultural systems, can help sequester carbon, reduce soil erosion, and provide a habitat for beneficial insects and wildlife. Similarly, the practice of intercropping, or growing multiple crops together, can increase the overall productivity of a plot while also improving soil health and reducing the need for chemical inputs.

Another critical aspect of permaculture is its focus on **closed-loop systems** that minimize waste and make the most of available resources. This approach reduces the environmental footprint of agricultural activities and helps address issues of food security and resource scarcity. For example, composting and vermiculture (worm farming) can transform organic waste into valuable fertilizer, reducing the need for synthetic inputs and diverting waste from landfills. Moreover, permaculture encourages the use of water-saving techniques, such as rainwater harvesting, swales, and mulching, which can help conserve water resources and adapt to changing precipitation patterns.

In addition to its direct environmental benefits, permaculture also has the potential to **foster social change** by promoting a more equitable and community-oriented approach to food production. By emphasizing local, small-scale, and diverse agricultural systems, permaculture can help counteract the negative impacts of industrial agriculture, such as the loss of traditional knowledge, the concentration of land ownership, and the marginalization of small-scale farmers. Furthermore, by encouraging community involvement and education, permaculture can empower individuals to take control of their food systems and become active agents of change.

In conclusion, permaculture offers a powerful and practical solution to many of the global environmental challenges we face today. By embracing its principles and practices, we can create more resilient and sustainable agricultural systems and foster a deeper connection with the natural world and our communities. As we look towards the future, it is clear that permaculture has a vital role to play in cultivating a more just, sustainable, and thriving planet for generations to come.

The Role of Technology and Innovation in Advancing Permaculture Practices

As we venture into the future, technology and innovation will play a crucial role in advancing permaculture practices. By harnessing the power of cutting-edge tools and techniques, we can optimize our efforts to create sustainable, resilient, and productive ecosystems that benefit both people and the planet.

One of the most promising areas of technological advancement is the field of **precision agriculture**. This approach uses data-driven insights and advanced monitoring systems to make more informed decisions about managing land, water, and other resources. By integrating these tools into permaculture practices, we can enhance our ability to observe, analyze, and respond to the unique needs of each site, ultimately leading to more efficient and effective systems.

For example, remote sensing technology, such as drones and satellite imagery, can provide valuable information about soil health, plant growth, and water usage. By analyzing this data, permaculture practitioners can identify patterns and trends that inform their design decisions, leading to more targeted interventions that maximize productivity while minimizing waste and environmental impact.

Another area of innovation is the development of new materials and techniques for **sustainable construction** and **infrastructure**. From green roofs and living walls to permeable paving and natural water filtration systems, these technologies offer exciting possibilities for integrating permaculture principles into the built environment. By embracing these innovations, we can create urban landscapes that support human well-being and contribute to the health and vitality of the ecosystems in which they are situated.

Furthermore, the rise of **digital communication** and **social media platforms** has created unprecedented opportunities for sharing knowledge, ideas, and best practices within the global permaculture community. By leveraging these tools, we can foster a spirit of collaboration and mutual learning that accelerates the spread of permaculture principles and techniques around the world.

Finally, it is important to recognize that technology and innovation are not just about the latest gadgets and gizmos. They also encompass the creative thinking and problem-solving skills that are at the heart of permaculture design. By cultivating a mindset of curiosity, experimentation, and adaptability, we can continually refine and improve our practices, ensuring that permaculture remains a dynamic and evolving discipline that is well-equipped to meet the challenges of the future.

In conclusion, the integration of technology and innovation into permaculture practices holds immense potential for enhancing the sustainability, resilience, and productivity of our ecosystems. By embracing these advancements and fostering a culture of continuous learning and improvement, we can ensure that permaculture remains at the forefront of efforts to create a more just, equitable, and ecologically sound world for future generations.

Fostering a Permaculture Mindset: Education and Community Involvement

As we have journeyed through the world of practical permaculture, it has become evident that the key to unlocking its full potential lies in fostering a permaculture mindset. This mindset, rooted in the principles of sustainability, resilience, and harmony with nature, can only be cultivated through education and community involvement. By spreading awareness and knowledge about permaculture practices, we can empower individuals and communities to take charge of their own food systems and contribute to a more sustainable future.

Education is the cornerstone of fostering a permaculture mindset. We can lay the foundation for a new generation of eco-conscious individuals by incorporating permaculture principles into school curriculums. Teaching children about the importance of soil health, water conservation, and biodiversity will instill a deep appreciation for the natural world and humans' role in preserving it. Furthermore, offering workshops and courses for adults can also broaden the reach of permaculture, equipping people with the skills and knowledge necessary to implement these practices in their own lives.

Community involvement is another essential aspect of nurturing a permaculture mindset. By creating spaces where people can come together to learn, share, and collaborate, we can foster a sense of unity and collective responsibility for the well-being of our planet. Community gardens, for example, serve as a tangible representation of permaculture principles in action, providing a platform for individuals to work together in cultivating a sustainable food system. These gardens not only produce fresh, local produce but also serve as a hub for learning and social interaction, strengthening the bonds between community members.

In addition to community gardens, local workshops, seminars, and conferences can also serve as opportunities for individuals to connect with like-minded people and learn from experts in the field. Community members can gain valuable insights and inspiration by engaging in these events to further their permaculture journey. Moreover, forming local permaculture groups or clubs can provide ongoing support and resources for those looking to deepen their understanding and practice of permaculture principles.

Ultimately, fostering a permaculture mindset is about more than just adopting specific techniques or practices. It is about embracing a holistic approach to living, one that recognizes the interconnectedness of all living systems and seeks to create harmony between human needs and the natural world. By prioritizing education and community involvement, we can cultivate a permaculture mindset that will not only benefit our immediate surroundings but also contribute to the global movement toward a more sustainable and resilient future.

Cultivating a Sustainable Future: The Lasting Legacy of Permaculture

As we stand at the precipice of a new era, it is crucial to recognize the importance of sustainable practices in shaping the future of our planet. With its emphasis on working in harmony with nature, permaculture offers a viable and promising solution to many of the challenges we face today. By embracing permaculture principles, we can cultivate a sustainable future that benefits both the environment and humanity.

The lasting legacy of permaculture lies in its ability to transform our relationship with the natural world. By adopting a holistic approach to agriculture, we can create self-sustaining ecosystems that provide for our needs while preserving the integrity of the environment. This shift in mindset, **from exploitation to stewardship**, can revolutionize how we interact with the earth and its resources.

Permaculture's impact extends beyond the realm of agriculture, as its principles can be applied to various aspects of our daily lives. From energy-efficient housing to waste reduction and water conservation, adopting permaculture practices can significantly reduce our ecological footprint and contribute to a more sustainable future.

Integrating technology and innovation in permaculture practices further enhances its potential to bring about lasting change. By harnessing the power of cutting-edge tools and techniques, we can optimize the efficiency of permaculture systems and maximize their positive impact on the environment. This marriage of traditional wisdom and modern innovation is a testament to the adaptability and resilience of permaculture as a solution for the challenges of the *21st century.*

Education and community involvement play a crucial role in fostering a permaculture mindset. By raising awareness about the principles of permaculture and their practical applications, we can inspire individuals and communities to take action toward a more sustainable future. This grassroots movement can create a ripple effect, spreading the message of permaculture far and wide and ultimately transforming how we live on this planet.

In conclusion, the future of permaculture is one of hope and promise. As we continue to face unprecedented environmental challenges, adopting sustainable practices like permaculture becomes increasingly vital. By embracing the principles of permaculture, we can cultivate a sustainable future that leaves a lasting legacy for generations to come. Together, we can work towards a world where humans and nature coexist in harmony, ensuring the health and well-being of our planet and all its inhabitants.

ABOUT THE AUTHOR

Michael Barton is an expert in sustainability and regenerative agriculture with over a decade of experience. He holds a degree in Environmental Studies and has received advanced training in the principles and practices of regenerative agriculture.

Throughout his career, Michael has worked with farmers, policymakers, and environmentalists to promote sustainable farming practices and advocate for the adoption of regenerative agriculture. He has collaborated with organizations worldwide to advance sustainable agriculture and food systems.

In his free time, Michael enjoys hiking and spending time with his family.

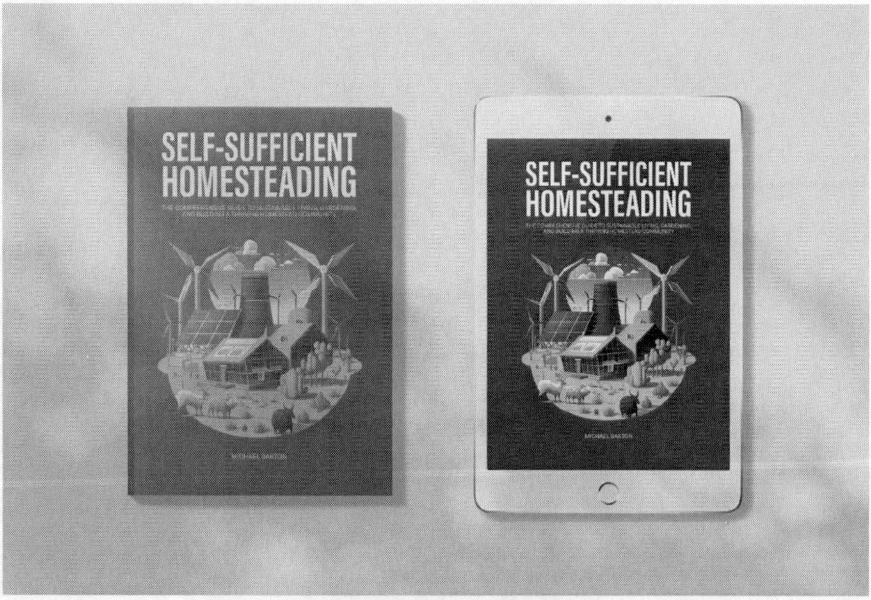

Manufactured by Amazon.ca
Acheson, AB

12479194R00085